Food Digest®

Favorite Brand Name Recipes

TORMONT

Everyday Broccoli Cheese Chicken (top), Skillet Herb-Roasted Chicken (recipes on page 82)

Food Digest®

Favorite Brand Name Recipes

KATHLEEN PERRY the everyday gourmet

Grateful acknowledgment is made to the companies and organizations listed below for the use of their recipes in this book.

Beef Industry Council and Beef Board
Campbell Soup Company
Con Agra Frozen Foods
The Creamette Company
Del Monte Foods
Durkee–French Foods
Florida Citrus Commission
General Mills, Inc.
H. J. Heinz Company
Hershey Foods Corporation
Geo. A. Hormel & Co.
Hunt–Wesson, Inc.
The HVR Company
Knox Gelatine, Inc.

Kraft General Foods Inc.
Land O'Lakes, Inc.
Lawry's® Foods, Inc.
Thomas J. Lipton, Inc.
Nabisco Foods Group
National Dairy Board
National Pork Producers Council
Nestlé Food Company
Old El Paso Foods Company
Pepperidge Farm, Inc.
The Quaker Oats Company
Uncle Ben's, Inc.
Van Den Bergh Foods Co.

Created and produced by Joshua Morris Publishing, Inc., 221 Danbury Rd., Wilton, CT 06897

Original photography for this book by Dennis M. Gottlieb.
How-to photography: Salvatore Maiuro.
Art director: Ann Beckstead.
Prop stylist: Adrienne Abseck.
Food stylist: Delores Custer.
Food stylist assistant: Hilary Huaman.

DESIGNED BY OPORORNIS AGILIS

Recipes previously appeared in the Food Digest® advertising section of Reader's Digest.

Published by Tormont Publications Inc.
338 Saint Antoine St. East
Montreal, Canada H2Y 1A3
Tel. (514) 954-1441
Fax (514) 954-5086

Copyright © 1994 Joshua Morris Publishing, Inc.
All rights reserved.
Printed in Canada.
No portion of this book may be reprinted or
reproduced in any form or manner without
the written permission of the publishers,
except by a reviewer who wishes to quote brief
passages in connection with a review.

10 9 8 7 6 5 4 3 2 1

ISBN: 2-89429-581-2

Contents

MEASUREMENTS

3 teaspoons = 1 tablespoon

4 tablespoons = ¼ cup

5 tablespoons plus 1 teaspoon = ⅓ cup

8 tablespoons = ½ cup

16 tablespoons = 1 cup

1 gallon = 4 quarts

½ gallon = 2 quarts

1 quart = 2 pints

1 pint = 2 cups

½ pint = 1 cup

1 cup = 8 ounces

1 ounce = 2 tablespoons

16 ounces = 1 pound

8 ounces = ½ pound

EQUIVALENTS

1 stick butter = ½ cup

2 sticks butter = 1 cup

1 pound butter = 2 cups

4 ounces (¼ pound) firm cheese

(Cheddar, Swiss) = 1 cup shredded

8 ounces cream cheese = 1 cup

5 large eggs = 1 cup

7 large egg whites = 1 cup

14 large egg yolks = 1 cup

5 ounces cooked, cubed chicken = 1 cup

1½ ounces sliced or diced mushrooms = 1 cup

6 graham crackers (5" x 2½") = 1 cup crumbs

24 vanilla wafers = 1 cup crumbs

SUBSTITUTIONS

2 tablespoons flour = 1 tablespoon cornstarch or arrowroot

1 cup sifted flour = 1 cup minus 2 tablespoons unsifted flour

1 cup cake flour = 1 cup minus 2 tablespoons sifted all-purpose flour

1 ounce semisweet chocolate = ½ ounce unsweetened chocolate plus 1 tablespoon sugar

1 ounce unsweetened chocolate = 3 tablespoons cocoa plus 1 tablespoon butter

1 cup buttermilk = 1 cup plain yogurt, or 1 tablespoon vinegar

(or lemon juice) plus enough milk to make 1 cup;

let stand 5 minutes.

1 medium clove garlic = ⅛ teaspoon garlic powder or ¾ teaspoon garlic salt

1 small onion = 1 teaspoon onion powder or 1 teaspoon minced dry onion

1 cup bread crumbs = ¾ cup cracker crumbs

INTRODUCTION

◆ This delicious collection of all-occasion recipes comes from the pages of the Food Digest. As the "everyday gourmet" and food consultant for Food Digest, it has been my pleasure to select these time-saving and easy-to-prepare favorites for you to make for your family and friends. All of the recipes were developed using quality brands you know and trust, and have been tested for accuracy, good taste, and ease of preparation. Beautiful photographs show off finished dishes to perfection.

◆ You'll love the easy-to-follow recipe format and step-by-step photos that simplify procedures and techniques. For handy reference, there's a chart of common measurements and equivalents as well as a list of ingredients to use for emergency substitutions. And don't miss my "everyday hints" in the back of the book. They'll make your life in the kitchen so much easier.

◆ What we set on the table is important, but equally significant is the hospitality and conviviality generated there. Even though we have more time-saving conveniences than our parents and grandparents, life today can still be complicated. We don't always have the time to do the things that matter most, and family life and friendships can sometimes become fragmented. Mealtime is frequently the only time we can be with those we care about. This book will help you make delicious meals while saving you time—precious time to enjoy those you love.

KATHLEEN PERRY
the everyday gourmet

Mexican Dip

MEXICAN DIP

2 envs. LIPTON Cream of
Chicken Flavor Cup-a-
Soup Instant Soup
¾ cup water
1 (4 oz.) can chopped green
chilies, drained
½ teaspoon chili powder
¾ cup shredded Cheddar
cheese

◆ In 1-quart casserole blend soup, water, chilies and chili powder. Microwave at high 4 minutes or until thickened.

◆ Stir in cheese and let stand, covered, 5 minutes or until cheese is melted. Stir; serve warm with corn chips.

◆ Conventional Directions: In small saucepan blend soup with water. Add remaining ingredients; simmer, stirring until cheese is melted.

Makes about 1½ cups dip.

QUICK 2-CHEESE PIZZA SNACKS

1 can refrigerated biscuits
¼ cup grated Parmesan
Cheese
1½ cups spaghetti or pizza
sauce
1 cup assorted toppings
(pepperoni, sautéed
mushrooms, peppers,
onions, etc.)
1½ cups shredded
mozzarella cheese

◆ Heat oven to 400°. Separate biscuits. Divide each biscuit in half crosswise for a thin, crisp crust.

◆ On an ungreased baking sheet, flatten each biscuit and crimp the edge to form a small ridge for the crust.

◆ Sprinkle Parmesan cheese over each biscuit. Spread sauce and toppings over Parmesan cheese. Top with mozzarella cheese.

◆ Bake 10 minutes on lowest rack until biscuits are lightly browned.

Makes 20 snacks.

Courtesy: National Dairy Board

Spicy Sausage Snacks, Appetizer Rounds

*S*PICY *S*AUSAGE *S*NACKS

1 (12 oz.) pkg. spicy ground
   pork sausage
2 cups BISQUICK® Original
   or Reduced Fat baking
   mix
1½ cups (6 oz.) shredded
   Cheddar cheese
¾ cup finely chopped
   green onions
½ cup grated Parmesan
   cheese
¼ cup sour cream
½ teaspoon garlic powder
⅔ cup milk
1 egg

◆ Heat oven to 350°. Grease 15½ x 10½ x 1-inch jellyroll pan. In 10-inch skillet cook sausage, stirring frequently, until brown; drain. (Note: sausage pieces should be the size of small peas.)

◆ In large bowl mix sausage and remaining ingredients; spread in pan.

◆ Bake 20 to 25 minutes or until golden brown. Cool 5 minutes; cut into 1½-inch squares. Serve warm.

Makes about 60.

APPETIZER ROUNDS

FOR CHEESY-ONION TOPPING:

⅓ cup mayonnaise or salad dressing

⅓ cup shredded Cheddar cheese

⅓ cup shredded mozzarella cheese

3 green onions (with tops), sliced

FOR ROUNDS:

2 cups BISQUICK® Original or Reduced Fat baking mix

¼ teaspoon garlic powder

½ cup boiling water*

◆ In small bowl combine topping ingredients; refrigerate. Heat oven to 400°.

◆ In medium bowl mix baking mix, garlic powder and water until soft dough forms. Let stand about 10 minutes or until cool.

◆ Turn onto surface dusted with baking mix; shape into ball. Knead 12 to 15 times or until smooth.

◆ Roll dough ⅛-inch thick. Cut with 2-inch round cutter dipped in baking mix.

◆ Place rounds about 1 inch apart on large, ungreased cookie sheet. Top each with about ½ teaspoon topping.

◆ Bake 10 to 12 minutes or until topping is golden brown. Immediately remove from cookie sheet. Serve hot.

Makes about 40.

(*Note: if using Reduced Fat baking mix, increase boiling water to ⅔ cup.)

BUFFALO-STYLE CHICKEN WINGS

12 chicken wings (about
    2 lbs.)
1 env. LIPTON Golden
    Onion Recipe Soup Mix
¼ cup butter or margarine,
    melted
1 tablespoon white vinegar
1 clove garlic
1½ teaspoons ground red
    pepper
½ teaspoon ground cumin
2 tablespoons water
1 cup WISH-BONE Chunky
    Blue Cheese Dressing

◆ Heat broiler. Cut tips off chicken wings. Halve the remaining wings at joint.

◆ In food processor or blender process soup mix, butter, vinegar, garlic, red pepper, cumin and water until blended; set aside.

◆ Broil chicken 5 minutes. Turn wings over; broil 5 more minutes.

◆ Brush with half the soup mixture, then broil 2 minutes or until crisp. Turn wings again and brush with remaining soup mixture. Broil 2 more minutes or until crisp. Serve with blue cheese dressing for dipping and chilled celery sticks.

Serves 4.

GOLDEN CHICKEN NUGGETS

1 env. LIPTON Golden
    Onion Recipe Soup Mix
¾ cup dry bread crumbs
1½ lbs. boneless chicken
    breasts, cut into 1-inch
    pieces
¼ cup butter or margarine,
    melted

◆ Heat oven to 400°. Combine onion soup mix with bread crumbs.

◆ Dip chicken into bread crumb mixture, coating well. Place in lightly greased, large shallow baking pan and drizzle with butter.

◆ Bake, turning once, 10 to 15 minutes or until chicken is tender.

Makes about 2 dozen.

Buffalo-Style Chicken Wings (top), Golden Chicken Nuggets

*P*EPPERONI *P*IZZA *S*OUP

1 (10¾ oz.) can
CAMPBELL'S® condensed
tomato soup
1 soup can water
⅓ cup sliced pepperoni
¼ teaspoon dried Italian
seasoning
¼ cup shredded mozzarella
cheese
½ cup croutons

◆ In 1½-quart saucepan stir soup. Gradually add water. Add pepperoni and Italian seasoning. Heat through over medium heat.

◆ Top with cheese and croutons.

Makes 2 servings.

*T*OMATO *T*ORTELLINI *S*OUP

1 (10¾ oz.) can
CAMPBELL'S® condensed
tomato soup
½ soup can water
½ soup can milk
⅓ teaspoon dried Italian
seasoning
½ cup frozen cheese
tortellini
2 tablespoons grated
Parmesan cheese

◆ In 1½-quart saucepan stir soup. Gradually add water and milk. Add Italian seasoning. Heat to simmering over medium heat.

◆ Add tortellini. Simmer 10 minutes, stirring occasionally.

◆ Garnish with Parmesan cheese.

Makes 2 servings.

Pepperoni Pizza Soup (top), Tomato Tortellini Soup

Corn and Ham Soup

CORN AND HAM SOUP

2 (13¾ oz.) cans chicken
  broth
1 (17 oz.) can DEL MONTE®
  Whole Kernel Golden
  Sweet Corn
1 cup diced ham
⅓ cup chopped onion
⅓ cup chopped green
  pepper
1 cup half-and-half

◆ In large saucepan combine all ingredients except half-and-half. Bring to boil; reduce heat. Cover and simmer 15 minutes.

◆ Stir in half-and-half; heat through.

Serves 6.

HEARTY SOUP

2 (13¾ oz.) cans chicken
  broth
3 cups tomato juice
1 (17 oz.) can DEL MONTE®
  Whole Kernel Golden
  Sweet Corn
1 (17 oz.) can DEL MONTE®
  Green Lima Beans
1 cup diced and cooked
  chicken
2 medium potatoes, pared
  and diced
1 medium onion, chopped
1 tablespoon
  Worcestershire sauce
1 teaspoon basil
¼ teaspoon pepper

◆ In large saucepan or soup pot combine all ingredients. Bring to boil; reduce heat. Cover and simmer 30 minutes or until potatoes are tender.

◆ Ladle into soup bowls.

Serves 6.

Herbed Stuffed Eggs

12 hard-cooked eggs
½ cup garlic and herb-cheese spread
¼ cup mayonnaise
¼ cup finely chopped scallions
2 tablespoons finely chopped pimientos
¼ cup GREY POUPON® Dijon or Country Dijon Mustard
Sliced scallions for garnish

◆ Halve eggs lengthwise. Scoop out yolks into a large bowl; set egg white halves aside.

◆ Mash yolks; blend in cheese spread, mayonnaise, scallions, pimientos and mustard until smooth.

◆ Spoon or pipe yolk mixture into egg white halves. Garnish with sliced scallions and serve.

Makes 24 appetizers.

Mushroom Puffs

3 tablespoons butter
1 lb. fresh mushrooms, cleaned and diced
1 small onion, finely chopped
24 oz. cream cheese, softened
2 egg yolks
3 tablespoons minced parsley
Salt and pepper to taste
Party bread slices
Paprika to taste

◆ In a medium-size skillet melt butter and sauté mushrooms and onion over medium heat until golden, stirring occasionally; drain.

◆ Heat broiler. In a medium-size bowl beat cream cheese, egg yolks, parsley and seasonings together until smooth. Stir in mushroom mixture until combined.

◆ Spread evenly on party bread slices and sprinkle with paprika. Broil 1 to 2 minutes or until lightly browned and puffed. Serve immediately.

Makes about 4 dozen canapés.

Courtesy: National Dairy Board

Creamy Dijon Topped Potatoes (center), Herbed Stuffed Eggs

CREAMY DIJON TOPPED POTATOES

1 (8 oz.) pkg. cream cheese, softened
¼ cup GREY POUPON® Dijon or Country Dijon Mustard
1 teaspoon dried basil leaves
⅓ cup finely chopped black olives
¼ cup finely chopped scallions
¼ cup finely chopped red pepper
18 small red skin potatoes, roasted and cut in half lengthwise
Scallion tips for garnish

◆ In medium bowl with electric mixer at medium speed beat cream cheese, mustard and basil until smooth. Stir in olives, scallions and red pepper.

◆ To serve, pipe or spoon 1 tablespoon mixture onto each potato half. Garnish with scallion tips and serve.

Makes 3 dozen appetizers.

Mock Mayo

1 large egg white
1 tablespoon vinegar
1 teaspoon Dijon Mustard
½ teaspoon sugar
  (optional)
¼ teaspoon salt
1 cup (8 oz.) low fat
  cotttage cheese

◆ In blender whip egg white, vinegar, mustard, sugar and salt one minute until light and frothy.

◆ With blender running, spoon in cottage cheese; blend until smooth. Refrigerate at least one hour before using.

Make 1 cup.

Courtesy: National Dairy Board

Cucumber-Dill Dressing/Dip

1 medium cucumber,
  peeled, cut in half
  lengthwise, seeded and
  finely chopped (1 cup)
1 cup Mock Mayo
2 tablespoons fresh dill
1 teaspoon lemon juice
½ clove garlic (optional)

◆ Prepare cucumber; set aside. Prepare Mock Mayo according to directions except add dill, lemon juice and garlic to egg white before blending in cottage cheese.

◆ Transfer mixture to a bowl. Squeeze excess water from cucumber; stir cucumber into dressing.

◆ Refrigerate at least one hour before using.

Make 2 cups.

Courtesy: National Dairy Board

Artichoke Dip (left), Cucumber-Dill Dressing/Dip

*A*RTICHOKE *D*IP

8 oz. canned artichokes, drained and finely chopped
12 oz. cream cheese, softened
½ stick butter, softened
2 tablespoons Parmesan cheese, grated
Small crackers

◆ Heat oven to 350°. In medium bowl mix together artichokes, cream cheese and butter.

◆ Place in a shallow baking dish; sprinkle Parmesan cheese on top.

◆ Bake for 20 minutes. Serve on small crackers.

Makes about 2 cups

Courtesy: National Dairy Board

Mock Herb Mayo Dressing/Dip

1 large egg white
1 tablespoon vinegar
1 teaspoon Dijon mustard
½ teaspoon sugar
   (optional)
¼ teaspoon salt
2 tablespoons chopped
   parsley
½ clove garlic
1 cup (8 oz.) low fat
   cottage cheese

◆ In blender whip egg white, vinegar, mustard, sugar, salt, parsley and garlic one minute until light and frothy.

◆ With blender running, spoon in cottage cheese; blend until smooth.

◆ Refrigerate at least one hour before using.

Makes 1 cup.

Courtesy: National Dairy Board

Parmesan-Peppercorn Dressing/Dip

1 cup Mock Herb Mayo
2 to 3 tablespoons
   Parmesan cheese
¼ teaspoon coarse ground
   pepper

◆ Prepare Mock Herb Mayo according to directions. Transfer mixture to bowl; stir in Parmesan cheese and pepper.

◆ Refrigerate at least one hour before using.

Makes 1 cup.

Courtesy: National Dairy Board

Macho Nacho

1 (15 oz.) can HORMEL Chili
   No Beans, heated
1 (8 oz.) bag tortilla chips,
   any flavor
½ cup shredded cheese
   (Cheddar, Jack or
   American)

◆ In shallow, microwaveable, 10-inch baking dish spoon chili over chips. Sprinkle with cheese.

◆ Place dish in microwave; heat on HIGH 3 minutes or until cheese is melted and bubbly. (Or, heat oven to 450°. Bake 10 minutes.)

Serves 4.

Macho Nacho

CREAMY PASTA VERDE

8 oz. fettuccine pasta
1 cup grated Romano
    cheese
1 cup shredded Monterey
    Jack cheese
1 (4 oz.) carton frozen
    pesto, thawed
2 cups sour cream
1 (16 oz.) can DEL MONTE®
    Blue Lake Cut Green
    Beans, drained
1 (17 oz.) can DEL MONTE®
    Sweet Peas, drained

◆ Cook pasta according to package directions; drain.

◆ Return pasta to pan. Toss with cheeses and pesto; heat gently until cheeses are melted. Fold in sour cream; heat through.

◆ Add vegetables; gently mix and heat thoroughly. Garnish with chopped parsley, if desired.

Makes 4 to 6 servings.

PASTA AND BEAN GRATIN

8 oz. pasta ruffles
3 cloves garlic, minced
1 small onion, finely
    chopped
2 tablespoons olive oil
2 tablespoons minced fresh
    basil
2 tablespoons minced fresh
    parsley
Salt and pepper to taste
1 (15 oz.) can white kidney
    beans, drained
1 (30 oz.) jar RAGÚ Chunky
    Gardenstyle Pasta
    Sauce—Chunky
    Mushrooms & Green
    Peppers
¼ cup grated Parmesan
    cheese
1 cup part-skim ricotta
    cheese
½ cup bread crumbs

◆ Cook pasta ruffles according to package directions. Drain and set aside.

◆ In large skillet sauté garlic and onion in olive oil until soft. Add seasonings and beans; sauté lightly.

◆ In large bowl thoroughly combine pasta sauce, pasta and Parmesan cheese with bean mixture. Pour into 11 x 7-inch baking dish. Drop ricotta cheese by spoonful onto pasta mixture. Sprinkle with bread crumbs.

◆ Heat oven to 350°. Bake 30 minutes or until bubbly. Serve.

Serves 6.

Creamy Pasta Verde

STUFFED SHELLS FLORENTINE

1 cup ricotta cheese

1 cup shredded mozzarella cheese

¼ cup grated Parmesan cheese

1 egg, slightly beaten

1 (10 oz.) pkg. frozen chopped spinach, cooked and well drained

½ teaspoon dried oregano leaves, crushed

¼ teaspoon salt

12 jumbo shell macaroni, cooked al dente, drained and cooled

1 (15½ oz.) jar PREGO® spaghetti sauce (1¾ cups)

◆ In bowl mix first 7 ingredients well. Stuff about 3 tablespoons cheese mixture into each shell.

◆ In 12 x 8-inch baking dish, spread ½ of the spaghetti sauce. Arrange shells, stuffed side up, in sauce. Spoon remaining sauce over shells. Cover with foil.

◆ Bake at 350° for 35 minutes or until hot. Sprinkle with chopped parsley.

Serves 4.

Tangy Tortellini Salad

1 (8 oz.) can HUNT'S®
Tomato Sauce

½ cup WESSON® vegetable
oil

⅓ cup red wine vinegar

½ teaspoon seasoned salt

¼ teaspoon garlic powder,
celery seed, pepper and
oregano

1 (7 oz.) box tortellini,
cooked according to
package directions,
rinsed and drained

1 cup julienne-cut ham or
salami

1 cup julienne-cut red bell
peppers

1 (3.5 oz.) can sliced ripe
olives, drained

¼ cup chopped red onions

Lettuce leaves

◆ In medium bowl whisk together first
8 ingredients. Cover and refrigerate until ready
to use.

◆ In large bowl mix tortellini, ham, bell peppers,
olives and onions.

◆ Arrange on lettuce leaves and top with dressing
before serving.

Makes 4 to 6 servings.

RISOTTO WITH SHRIMP AND SWEET PEPPERS

1 red bell pepper, diced
1 yellow bell pepper, diced
2 large cloves garlic,
   minced
3 tablespoons olive oil,
   divided
1 (27½ oz.) jar RAGÚ
   Today's Recipe Pasta
   Sauce—Garden Harvest
3 (13¾ oz.) cans low-salt
   chicken broth
1½ cups Arborio rice
1 lb. large shrimp, peeled
   and deveined
⅓ cup grated Parmesan
   cheese

◆ In large skillet sauté red and yellow peppers and garlic in 2 tablespoons olive oil; set aside.

◆ In large saucepan combine pasta sauce with chicken broth; heat thoroughly.

◆ In Dutch oven or stockpot lightly sauté rice in remaining olive oil. Add about 1 cup heated sauce mixture to rice.

◆ Cook over low to medium heat at a very low simmer, stirring frequently. Continue adding hot sauce mixture gradually. Stir and cook about 30 to 40 minutes or until rice is tender.

◆ During last 5 minutes of cooking add shrimp to skillet with peppers; sauté until shrimp just turn pink. Stir Parmesan cheese into risotto. (Rice should be moist and creamy.)

◆ Spoon hot risotto into a large serving bowl. Top with shrimp and peppers.

Serves 8.

GREEK PASTA

½ of a (1 lb.) pkg.
   CREAMETTE® Fettuccini,
   uncooked
⅓ cup olive oil
2 cloves garlic, minced
2 medium ripe tomatoes,
   peeled, seeded and
   chopped
½ cup ripe pitted olives,
   cut in wedges
4 oz. Feta cheese, crumbled
½ teaspoon dried oregano
Freshly ground black
   pepper to taste
Salt to taste

◆ Prepare fettuccine according to package directions; drain.

◆ Meanwhile, in medium skillet heat oil and garlic. Stir in remaining ingredients, except fettuccini; simmer 5 minutes.

◆ Arrange hot fettuccini on warm serving platter. Top with tomato mixture. Serve immediately.

Makes 4 servings.

TUSCAN-STYLE FETTUCCINE WITH ARTICHOKES

1 lb. fettuccine
½ cup (1 stick) I CAN'T
   BELIEVE IT'S NOT
   BUTTER!®
1 (14 oz.) can artichoke
   hearts, drained and
   chopped
⅓ cup chopped fresh
   cilantro
2 tablespoons chopped
   fresh oregano, or
   1 tablespoon dried
2 tablespoons minced
   garlic
½ teaspoon pepper
2 to 3 cups freshly grated
   Parmesan cheese

◆ Cook fettuccine "al dente" according to package directions; drain. Keep warm and set aside.

◆ In large skillet over medium-high heat melt I Can't Believe It's Not Butter! Add artichokes, cilantro, oregano, garlic and pepper.

◆ Cook, stirring, for several minutes until ingredients are combined and mixture is hot. Pour over warm pasta and toss to coat evenly.

◆ Divide onto hot plates, sprinkle generously with Parmesan cheese and serve.

Makes 6 servings.

CONFETTI VEGETABLE PASTA

1 (28 oz.) jar RAGÚ Slow-Cooked Homestyle Spaghetti Sauce—Tomato and Herbs

1 clove garlic, minced

2 tablespoons olive oil

1 cup *each* chopped fresh broccoli and shredded carrots

1 *each* small red pepper, zucchini and yellow squash, diced

1 (12 oz.) pkg. twist or ruffle pasta, cooked and drained

1 tablespoon garlic-herb cheese spread

2 tablespoons shredded Parmesan cheese

1 tablespoon chopped fresh parsley

◆ In medium saucepan thoroughly heat sauce; set aside.

◆ In large, non-stick skillet, over medium heat, sauté garlic in olive oil. Add vegetables. Sauté, stirring frequently, about 5 minutes or until tender-crisp.

◆ Toss hot pasta with garlic-herb and Parmesan cheese. Spoon heated sauce over pasta; toss to coat well. Top pasta with sautéed vegetables. Sprinkle with parsley.

Serves 6.

FOUR-CHEESE LASAGNA

3 cups (30 oz.) ricotta cheese

1 cup mozzarella cheese, divided

½ cup grated Parmesan cheese

½ cup grated Romano cheese

2 eggs, lightly beaten

2 tablespoons chopped parsley

9 (8 oz.) lasagna noodles

1 lb. ground meat

3 cups spaghetti sauce

◆ In large bowl combine ricotta, ½ cup mozzarella, Parmesan and Romano cheeses, eggs and parsley; set aside.

◆ In large rectangular pan soak uncooked lasagna noodles in cold water for 10 minutes to soften slightly; drain.

◆ In skillet over medium heat cook ground meat until lightly browned; drain. In large bowl place spaghetti sauce; stir meat into sauce.

◆ Heat oven to 350°. In 8 x 12-inch glass baking dish spread ½ cup sauce. Place 3 lasagna noodles side by side over sauce. Spread ⅓ ricotta filling over noodles. Spread 1 cup sauce over filling.

◆ Repeat layers with remaining ingredients, ending with sauce.

◆ Cover tightly with aluminum foil and bake 1 hour. Remove foil, top with remaining mozzarella cheese and bake 3 minutes until cheese has melted.

◆ Remove from oven and allow to stand at least 10 minutes before cutting.

Makes 6 to 8 servings.

Courtesy: National Dairy Board

Soak uncooked lasagna noodles in cold water to soften slightly.

Place 3 noodles side by side on top of first layer of sauce.

Dot noodles with spoonfuls of ricotta filling; spread with spatula. Cover with sauce.

ᏢASTA PRIMAVERA

1 cup thinly sliced carrots
1 large clove garlic, minced
¼ cup olive oil
1 (14½ oz.) can DEL
    MONTE® Original Style
    Stewed Tomatoes
2 cups sliced mushrooms
2 tablespoons cornstarch
2 teaspoons crushed basil
½ teaspoon crushed
    oregano
1 (16 oz.) can DEL MONTE®
    Blue Lake Cut Green
    Beans, drained
8 oz. rigatoni, cooked and
    drained
¼ cup grated Parmesan
    cheese
1 tablespoon chopped
    parsley (optional)

◆ In large skillet sauté carrots and garlic in olive oil over medium-low heat until carrots are tender-crisp, about 5 minutes.

◆ Stir in tomatoes, mushrooms, cornstarch and herbs. Cook, stirring constantly, until thickened and translucent.

◆ Add beans; heat through. Add pasta to skillet; toss with cheese. Garnish with chopped parsley, if desired.

Makes 4 to 6 servings.

SPINACH LASAGNA

2 cups lowfat cottage
  cheese (1% milkfat)
2 (10 oz.) pkgs. frozen
  chopped spinach,
  defrosted and well
  drained
½ cup EGG BEATERS®
  99% Real Egg Product
1 teaspoon Italian
  seasoning
2 cups no-salt-added
  spaghetti sauce, divided
9 cooked lasagna noodles,
  prepared without added
  salt, divided
1 cup shredded part-skim
  mozzarella cheese (about
  4 oz.)
3 tablespoons grated
  Parmesan cheese

◆ In medium bowl combine cottage cheese, spinach, egg product and Italian seasoning; set aside.

◆ Spread ½ cup spaghetti sauce in bottom of greased 13 x 9 x 2-inch baking dish.

◆ Layer ⅓ each of noodles, spinach filling and remaining sauce; repeat twice. Sprinkle top with mozzarella cheese and Parmesan cheese; cover.

◆ Heat oven to 375°. Bake 20 minutes. Uncover; bake 25 minutes more. Let stand 10 minutes before serving.

Makes 8 servings.

HEARTY DEEP DISH PIZZA

1 loaf frozen bread dough, thawed to room temperature

1 (8 oz.) ball HEALTHY CHOICE® Fat Free natural Mozzarella Cheese, thinly sliced

1 cup HEALTHY CHOICE® Pasta Sauce

1 clove garlic, minced

1 teaspoon crushed dried oregano leaves

1 teaspoon crushed dried basil leaves

1 small onion, cut into rings (about 1 cup)

½ large green pepper, seeded and cut into strips

1 cup fresh mushroom slices

1 (8 oz.) pkg. HEALTHY CHOICE® Fat Free natural Fancy Shredded Pizza Cheese

◆ Heat oven to 450°. Press bread dough onto bottom and 1 inch up sides of 13 x 9-inch baking pan that has been sprayed with non-stick cooking spray.

◆ Bake 10 minutes. Remove from oven. Top with mozzarella cheese.

◆ In small bowl combine pasta sauce, garlic, oregano and basil; spread over cheese.

◆ Top with onion, green pepper and mushrooms; sprinkle with shredded pizza cheese. Continue baking 10 to 15 minutes or until cheese melts and crust is deep golden brown.

Makes 12 servings.

VEGETABLE GARDEN MANICOTTI

1 (16 oz.) container non-fat cottage cheese

1 (10 oz.) pkg. frozen chopped spinach, thawed and squeezed dry

2 cups HEALTHY CHOICE® Fat Free natural shredded Mozzarella Cheese, divided

1 cup shredded carrot

1 cup shredded zucchini

◆ In medium bowl combine cottage cheese, spinach, 1 cup mozzarella cheese, carrot, zucchini, egg product, garlic powder and pepper.

◆ Heat oven to 350°. Spoon mixture into manicotti shells, using a scant ⅓ cup per shell.

◆ Cover bottom of greased 13 x 9 x 2-inch baking dish with half of the pasta sauce. Place filled manicotti shells in a single layer.

(continued)

¼ cup HEALTHY CHOICE®
  Cholesterol-Free Egg
  Product
¼ teaspoon garlic powder
⅛ teaspoon pepper
1 (8 oz.) pkg. manicotti
  shells, cooked and
  drained
1 (26 oz.) jar HEALTHY
  CHOICE® Traditional
  Pasta Sauce
2 tablespoons grated
  Parmesan cheese

◆ Pour remaining pasta sauce over shells; sprinkle with remaining mozzarella and Parmesan cheeses.

◆ Bake covered 30 to 40 minutes or until hot and bubbly. Remove cover during last 10 minutes of baking.

Makes 7 servings.

Hearty Deep Dish Pizza (left), Vegetable Garden Manicotti

Summer Pasta Salad

1½ cups medium pasta shells, cooked and cooled
1½ cups fusilli pasta, cooked and cooled
1 cup julienne ham
½ cup sliced pimiento-stuffed green olives
½ cup *each* red, yellow and green bell pepper strips
¼ cup thinly sliced red onion
6 tablespoons olive oil
¼ cup HEINZ Apple Cider, Distilled White or Specialty Vinegar
Salt and pepper
2 heads Boston lettuce, separated into leaves, washed and dried

◆ Place pasta in medium mixing bowl; add ham, olives, peppers and onion.

◆ Stir in oil and vinegar. Season to taste. Serve on a bed of lettuce in salad bowl, either chilled or at room temperature.

Makes 4 to 6 servings.

Sausage Linguine Pie

½ of a (1 lb.) pkg.
  CREAMETTE® Linguine,
  uncooked
½ lb. Italian sausage,
  removed from its casing
1 (14 to 16 oz.) jar prepared
  spaghetti sauce, divided
2 eggs, beaten
1 cup ricotta cheese
1 (10 oz.) pkg. frozen
  chopped spinach, thawed
  and well drained
½ teaspoon salt
Grated Parmesan cheese

◆ Heat oven to 350°. Prepare linguine according to package directions; drain.

◆ Meanwhile, in medium skillet over medium heat cook sausage until no longer pink. Break the meat into small pieces; drain. Stir in 1 cup spaghetti sauce. In medium bowl blend remaining spaghetti sauce and eggs. Add linguine; toss to coat.

◆ Spread linguine mixture on bottom and sides of a greased 9-inch pie plate, forming a small rim.

◆ In small bowl combine ricotta, spinach and salt; mix well. Spread evenly in linguine shell. Top with meat mixture.

◆ Bake until hot, about 30 minutes. Sprinkle with Parmesan cheese. Let stand 5 minutes before cutting.

Makes 6 servings.

Spread linguine mixture on the bottom and sides of pie plate. Use back of spoon to form a small rim.

Spread the ricotta and spinach mixture evenly over the linguine.

Top with spaghetti sauce mixture.

PENNE WITH CHICKEN STRIPS AND BROCCOLI

2 tablespoons plus ½ cup I CAN'T BELIEVE IT'S NOT BUTTER!®, softened and divided
3 boneless chicken breast halves (about ¾ lb.), sliced into strips
¼ cup flour
Freshly ground pepper to taste
1 clove garlic, peeled and minced (optional)
¾ lb. penne (or any short tubular pasta such as ziti or rigatoni)
4 cups broccoli florets and peeled stems, cut into bite-size pieces
1 cup grated Parmesan cheese

◆ In large skillet over medium heat melt 2 tablespoons I Can't Believe It's Not Butter!

◆ On sheet of wax paper lightly coat chicken in flour and pepper; shake off any excess. Immediately place chicken in hot skillet; sauté 2 minutes, stirring frequently until just browned on both sides. Stir in garlic; cook 1 minute longer. Do not let garlic brown. Cover and keep warm.

◆ In large pot bring 5 quarts of water to a rolling boil. Add pasta; cook uncovered 6 minutes. Carefully add broccoli; continue cooking until pasta is al dente. Reserve 1 cup cooking water before draining pasta.

◆ Meanwhile, in large serving bowl, blend cheese with remaining I Can't Believe It's Not Butter! until fluffy.

◆ Blend with reserved cooking water to make a sauce. Add pasta, chicken and broccoli; gently toss until combined. Serve with additional cheese and add pepper to taste, if desired.

Serves 4 to 6.

Mexi-Mac Casserole

1 (7 oz.) pkg. CREAMETTE® Elbow Macaroni (2 cups uncooked)
1 (15 oz.) can HORMEL Chili No Beans
¼ cup tomato juice
1 (4 oz.) can diced green chilies
¼ cup sliced green onions
1½ cups (6 oz.) shredded Cheddar cheese, divided
2 cups tortilla chips, divided
½ cup sour cream
1 medium tomato, chopped
1 tablespoon chopped cilantro

◆ Prepare macaroni according to package directions; drain. In medium saucepan heat chili, tomato juice, green chilies and green onions.

◆ Combine macaroni, chili mixture and ½ cup cheese. Crush 1 cup tortilla chips and spread on bottom of a 3-quart baking dish. Spoon in macaroni mixture. Top with remaining tortilla chips and cheese.

◆ Heat oven to 350°. Bake 30 minutes. Garnish top with sour cream, tomato and cilantro.

◆ Refrigerate leftovers.

Makes 6 to 8 servings.

SPAGHETTI WITH LEAN MEATBALLS

1 lb. ground turkey
1 egg, lightly beaten
½ cup Italian seasoned
    bread crumbs
2 tablespoons minced fresh
    parsley
1 small clove garlic, minced
    (optional)
⅛ teaspoon black pepper
1 tablespoon olive oil
1 (27½ oz.) jar RAGÚ
    Today's Recipe Pasta
    Sauce—Tomato Herb
12 oz. spaghetti
Grated Parmesan cheese
    (optional)

◆ In large bowl thoroughly combine ground turkey, egg, bread crumbs, parsley, garlic and pepper. Shape into 1½-inch meatballs.

◆ In large, non-stick skillet over medium heat, brown meatballs on all sides in olive oil. Drain fat.

◆ Reduce heat to low, add pasta sauce; cover and simmer 30 minutes or until meatballs are completely cooked.

◆ Meanwhile, cook pasta according to package directions; drain. Ladle sauce and meatballs over hot spaghetti. Sprinkle with cheese.

Serves 6.

FOOLPROOF BEEF & BROCCOLI

¾ lb. boneless beef sirloin
    steak, sliced across the
    grain into very thin strips
1 clove garlic, minced
1 tablespoon vegetable oil
1 medium onion, cut into
    wedges
1 (10¾ oz.) can
    CAMPBELL'S® Cream of
    Broccoli Soup
¼ cup water
1 tablespoon soy sauce
2 cups broccoli florets
Hot cooked noodles

◆ In skillet over medium-high heat cook beef and garlic in hot oil until beef is browned. Add onion; cook 5 minutes, stirring often.

◆ Stir in soup, water and soy sauce. Heat to boiling. Add broccoli. Reduce heat to low. Cover and simmer 5 minutes or until vegetables are crisp-tender.

◆ Serve over noodles.

Makes 4 servings.

CHEESY BEEF 'N' MAC BAKE

½ lb. ground beef
½ cup chopped onion
1 (11⅛ oz.) can
    CAMPBELL'S® condensed
    Italian tomato soup
¾ cup water
⅛ teaspoon pepper
2 cups cooked elbow
    macaroni (1 cup dry)
1 cup shredded Cheddar
    cheese (4 oz.), divided

◆ Heat oven to 400°. In 10-inch skillet over medium-high heat cook beef and onion until beef is browned and onion is tender, stirring to separate meat. Spoon off fat.

◆ Stir in soup, water, pepper, macaroni and ½ cup Cheddar cheese.

◆ Spoon mixture into 1½-quart casserole. Top with remaining cheese.

◆ Bake 25 minutes or until hot and bubbling.

Makes 4½ cups or 4 servings.

Foolproof Beef & Broccoli

PEPPERED BEEF KABOBS

2 tablespoons vegetable oil
1 tablespoon *each* fresh
   lemon juice and water
2 teaspoons Dijon-style
   mustard
1 teaspoon honey
½ teaspoon dried oregano
   leaves
¼ teaspoon pepper
1 lb. boneless beef sirloin
   steak, cut into 1-inch
   pieces, 1 inch thick
1 medium green, red or
   yellow bell pepper,
   trimmed, seeded and cut
   into 1-inch pieces
8 large mushrooms
Salt to taste (optional)

◆ Heat broiler. In large bowl whisk together oil, lemon juice, water, mustard, honey, oregano and pepper. Add beef, bell pepper and mushrooms, tossing to coat.

◆ Alternately thread pieces of beef, bell pepper and mushrooms on each of 4 12-inch skewers.

◆ Place kabobs on rack in broiler pan so surface of meat is 3 to 4 inches from heat. Broil 9 to 12 minutes for rare to medium, turning occasionally. Season with salt, if desired. (Or, prepare grill; place kabobs on grid over medium coals. Grill 8 to 11 minutes.)

Makes 4 servings.

Courtesy: Beef Industry Council and Beef Board

Mexican Beef Stir Fry

2 tablespoons vegetable oil
1 teaspoon *each* ground
   cumin and dried oregano
   leaves
1 clove garlic, minced
1 red or green bell pepper,
   trimmed, seeded and cut
   into thin strips
1 medium onion, cut into
   thin wedges
1 to 2 jalapeño peppers,
   thinly sliced (remove
   interior ribs and seeds if
   a milder flavor is desired)
1 lb. beef flank steak, cut
   into ⅛-inch-thick strips
3 cups thinly sliced lettuce

◆ In small bowl combine oil, cumin, oregano and garlic; reserve half.

◆ In large, non-stick skillet warm half the seasoned oil over medium-high heat. Add bell pepper, onion and jalapeño pepper; stir-fry 2 to 3 minutes or until crisp-tender. Remove; set aside.

◆ In same skillet stir-fry beef strips, half at a time, over medium-high heat in remaining oil 1 to 2 minutes.

◆ Return vegetables to skillet, toss with beef and heat through. Serve beef mixture over lettuce.

Makes 4 servings.

Courtesy: Beef Industry Council and Beef Board

Roasted Peppers With Chili

1 lb. poblano or ancho
   chilies or bell peppers
½ lb. sliced Oacaca,
   asadero or Monterey Jack
   cheese
1 (15 oz.) can HORMEL®
   Chili With Beans
Hot cooked rice
¼ cup chopped cilantro

◆ Place chilies in heavy 10-inch skillet (preferably cast-iron); cover. Cook over high heat 12 to 15 minutes, turning occasionally, or until skin chars on all sides.

◆ Place in plastic bag; let stand 5 minutes. When cool enough to handle, remove stem, seeds and skin.

◆ Stuff roasted chilies with cheese. Return chilies to skillet. Add chili. Cook over medium heat 6 to 8 minutes, stirring occasionally, until simmering.

◆ Arrange chilies with chili on rice. Garnish with cilantro and serve.

Serves 4.

Chili Corn Soufflé (top), Roasted Peppers with Chili (page 47)

CHILI CORN SOUFFLÉ

1 (15 oz.) can HORMEL Chili No Beans
1½ cups seeded, chopped tomatoes
½ cup sliced green onions
1 (8¾ oz.) can cream-style corn
¼ cup mayonnaise
¼ teaspoon crushed red pepper flakes
6 eggs, separated
½ teaspoon cream of tartar
1½ cups (6 oz.) shredded Cheddar cheese

◆ Grease a 15½ x 10½ x 1-inch jellyroll pan; line with wax paper, extending 3 inches beyond pan on each end. Grease and lightly flour wax paper.

◆ In small saucepan combine chili, tomatoes and green onions; cook over low heat until thoroughly heated. Set aside.

◆ In small saucepan combine corn, mayonnaise and red pepper; cook over low heat until thoroughly heated, stirring constantly. Remove from heat.

◆ Heat oven to 350°. In large bowl of an electric mixer beat egg yolks until thick and lemon colored. Gradually stir corn mixture into yolks.

◆ In large bowl beat egg whites at high speed with electric mixer until foamy. Add cream of tartar; beat until stiff but not dry. Fold beaten egg whites into yolk mixture. Pour into prepared pan, spreading evenly.

◆ Bake 15 to 20 minutes or until set. Loosen edges of soufflé with metal spatula, but do not remove from pan. Place a piece of wax paper longer than jellyroll pan over soufflé. Place inverted baking sheet over wax paper. Invert soufflé; remove jellyroll pan; carefully peel off wax paper. Sprinkle cheese over surface; roll up soufflé, using wax paper to support it. Place on serving platter; keep warm.

◆ Reheat chili mixture and spoon over soufflé slices.

Makes 6 to 8 servings.

Courtesy: Geo. A. Hormel & Company

TACO SALAD

1 lb. ground beef
1 pouch CAMPBELL'S® dry onion quality soup and recipe mix
½ cup water
2 tablespoons chili powder
6 cups torn salad greens
Tortilla chips (about 3 cups)
1 medium tomato, chopped
1 cup shredded Cheddar cheese (4 oz.)
6 fresh cilantro sprigs

◆ In 10-inch skillet, over medium heat, cook beef until browned and no longer pink, stirring to separate meat. Spoon off fat.

◆ Stir in soup mix, water and chili powder. Heat to boiling. Reduce heat to low. Cook 10 minutes, stirring occasionally.

◆ To serve, arrange lettuce on platter. Spoon hot meat mixture over lettuce. Top with chips, tomato and cheese. (Additional toppings may include sliced green onions and sliced, pickled jalapeño peppers. Serve sour cream on the side.) Garnish with cilantro, if desired.

Makes 6 servings.

FRENCH COUNTRY-STYLE BEEF STEW

1½ lbs. stew beef, cut in
   1-inch cubes
¼ cup flour
2 tablespoons oil
2 (14½ oz.) cans DEL
   MONTE® Original Style
   Stewed Tomatoes
1 (13¾ oz.) can beef broth
4 medium carrots, pared
   and cut in 1-inch chunks
2 medium potatoes, pared
   and cut in 1-inch chunks
¾ teaspoon thyme
2 tablespoons Dijon
   mustard (optional)

◆ Combine meat and flour in a plastic bag; toss to coat evenly.

◆ In 6-quart pot brown meat in oil. Add salt and pepper to taste, if desired.

◆ Add remaining ingredients except mustard. Bring to a boil; reduce heat.

◆ Cover and simmer one hour or until beef is tender. Stir occasionally.

◆ Blend in mustard. Garnish with chopped parsley and serve.

Serves 6 to 8.

Place 2 tablespoons of flour in plastic bag. Add approximately ⅓ of the meat cubes.

Toss the beef to coat evenly. Tapping the bottom of the bag will help to ensure that the meat is completely coated.

Brown meat in oil. Stir with a wooden spatula to prevent the meat from sticking or burning.

ITALIAN BEEF STIR-FRY

1 lb. beef round tip steaks, cut ⅛ to ¼ inch thick or 1 lb. beef strips for stir-fry
2 cloves garlic, crushed
1 tablespoon olive oil
2 small zucchini, thinly sliced
1 cup cherry tomato halves
¼ cup reduced-calorie bottled Italian salad dressing
2 cups hot cooked spaghetti
1 tablespoon grated Parmesan cheese

◆ Cut beefsteaks crosswise into 1-inch-wide strips; cut each strip crosswise in half; set aside.

◆ In large nonstick skillet over medium-high heat cook and stir garlic in oil 1 minute.

◆ Add beef strips, half at a time; stir-fry 1 to 1½ minutes. Season with salt and pepper, if desired. Remove with slotted spoon; keep warm.

◆ Add zucchini to same skillet; stir-fry 2 to 3 minutes or until crisp-tender. Return beef to skillet with tomato halves and dressing; heat through.

◆ Pour beef mixture over hot pasta; sprinkle with Parmesan cheese.

Makes 4 servings.

Courtesy: Beef Industry Council and Beef Board

FRENCH BEEF AU GRATIN

½ cup (1 stick) I CAN'T
BELIEVE IT'S NOT
BUTTER!®
4 cups thinly sliced Vidalia
or white onions
1 lb. beef tenderloin or
sirloin, sliced into ½-inch
cubes
3 tablespoons flour
1 tablespoon dark brown
sugar, packed
1 teaspoon cumin
1 teaspoon salt
½ teaspoon pepper
1 qt. beef broth
2 cups cooked fettuccine
1 cup (4 oz.) shredded
mozzarella cheese
½ cup grated Parmesan
cheese

◆ In large, heavy-bottomed pan over medium heat, melt I Can't Believe It's Not Butter! Add onions; sauté, stirring often, until caramelized but not burned, 15 to 20 minutes.

◆ With slotted spoon remove onions to medium bowl. Add beef to pan; brown well on all sides. Return onions and any juices to pan.

◆ In small bowl mix flour, sugar, cumin, salt and pepper. Add to pan; stir 1 minute until bubbly. Gradually add broth, stirring to scrape drippings from pan; simmer 10 minutes.

◆ Heat broiler. Place ½ cup fettuccine in each of 4 (about 16 oz.) ovenproof bowls; divide beef mixture over pasta.

◆ In medium bowl stir cheeses together; sprinkle evenly over beef. Broil until cheese is melted and lightly browned, about 5 minutes.

Makes 4 servings.

GOLDEN GLAZED FLANK STEAK

1 env. LIPTON Onion Recipe
   Soup Mix
1 (12 oz.) jar apricot
   preserves
½ cup water
1 flank steak (about 2 lbs.),
   cut into thin strips
2 medium peppers (green,
   red or yellow), cut into
   thin vertical slices
Hot cooked rice

◆ Heat broiler. In small bowl combine soup mix, apricot preserves and water. Mix well.

◆ In large shallow baking pan arrange steak and peppers; spoon soup mixture evenly on top.

◆ Broil, turning once, until steak is done to taste. Serve over hot rice.

Serves 6 to 8.

PRIME RIB WITH MUSTARD SAUCE

1 (5 to 6 lb.) standing rib
   roast
1 clove garlic, minced
1 teaspoon salt
1 teaspoon paprika
½ cup mayonnaise
¼ cup GREY POUPON®
   Dijon Mustard
¼ cup prepared
   horseradish

◆ Heat oven to 475°. Rub meat with garlic and sprinkle with salt and paprika.

◆ Place meat in uncovered roasting pan, fat side up. Cook 30 minutes or until browned.

◆ Reduce temperature to 325° and cook until meat is tender, allowing 30 minutes per pound for medium-well and 18 minutes per pound for rare meat.

◆ Meanwhile, in small bowl combine mayonnaise, mustard and horseradish; mix well. Serve with meat.

Makes 6 servings plus 1 cup sauce.

VEAL SAUSAGE AND PEPPER POLENTA

FOR POLENTA:
4 cups water
1 cup cornmeal
1 teaspoon salt

FOR TOPPING:
1 lb. veal sausage, thickly
   sliced
2 tablespoons olive oil
2 cloves garlic, minced
2 red or green bell peppers,
   trimmed, seeded and
   diced
1 (27½ oz.) jar RAGÚ
   Today's Recipe Pasta
   Sauce—Chunky
   Mushroom

◆ In large saucepan bring water to a boil. Slowly mix in cornmeal and salt, stirring constantly, until mixture boils. Reduce heat to low and simmer 20 minutes, stirring frequently.

◆ Evenly spread polenta in lightly greased, 9x13-inch jellyroll pan. Cool completely.

◆ In large skillet thoroughly brown veal sausage in olive oil. Remove and set aside.

◆ In same skillet sauté garlic and peppers until tender. Return sausage to skillet; add pasta sauce. Simmer covered 20 minutes over low heat.

◆ Heat oven to 375°. Cut polenta into 8 squares. Place in large, shallow baking pan. Spoon sausage and pepper mixture evenly over polenta.

◆ Bake 20 minutes or until heated through.

Serves 8.

Prime Rib with Mustard Sauce

$\mathcal{V}$EAL SCALOPPINE WITH LEMON AND CAPERS

¼ cup flour
¼ teaspoon black pepper
8 veal scallops (about 1 lb.)
3 tablespoons I CAN'T
  BELIEVE IT'S NOT
  BUTTER!®
½ cup beef broth
2 tablespoons lemon juice
2 tablespoons capers,
  drained

◆ Combine flour and pepper on a plate. Press the veal pieces into the mixture coating them all over and shaking off any excess.

◆ In heavy, 10-inch skillet, over moderately high heat, melt I Can't Believe It's Not Butter! until the foam subsides, about 1 minute. Add the veal and brown quickly, about 1 minute on each side; do not overcook. As each piece of veal is cooked, transfer it to a heated platter.

◆ Add broth to the skillet, scraping up any browned bits on the bottom. Cook until slightly reduced and thickened, about 1 minute. Stir in the lemon juice and capers. Reduce heat to low.

◆ Return the veal and any accumulated juices to the skillet. Heat through, turning them over once.

◆ Arrange the veal pieces on platter and spoon sauce over them.

Serves 4.

PORK CHOP AND CORN STUFFING BAKE

1 (10¾ oz.) can
CAMPBELL'S® condensed
golden corn soup
¼ cup finely chopped
celery
¼ cup finely chopped
onion
½ teaspoon paprika
1½ cups PEPPERIDGE
FARM® corn bread
stuffing

◆ In medium bowl combine soup, celery, onion, paprika and stuffing.

◆ In 9-inch greased pie plate spoon stuffing mixture. Arrange chops over mixture, pressing lightly into stuffing.

◆ In cup combine sugar and mustard. Mix into a paste, then spread evenly over chops.

◆ Heat oven to 400°. Bake 30 minutes or until chops are no longer pink.

(continued)

4 boneless pork chops,
¾ inch thick (about 1 lb.),
well trimmed of fat
1 tablespoon packed
brown sugar
1 teaspoon spicy brown
mustard

◆ Transfer chops to serving platter. Stir stuffing; serve with chops.

Makes 2¼ cups stuffing or 4 servings.

Use a spatula or spoon to spread the stuffing mixture evenly in a greased pie plate.

Lightly press the chops into the stuffing mixture.

Brush the sugar and mustard paste evenly over the chops.

Spicy Pork Chop Bake

6 pork chops, 1 inch thick
(about 2½ lbs.)
1 (11⅛ oz.) can
CAMPBELL'S® condensed
Italian tomato soup
2 tablespoons water
2 tablespoons vinegar
1 tablespoon packed
brown sugar
1 tablespoon
Worcestershire sauce
¼-½ teaspoon hot pepper
sauce or to taste

◆ Heat oven to 400°. In 3-quart, oblong baking dish arrange chops in single layer.

◆ Bake 20 minutes or until chops begin to brown. Spoon off fat.

◆ Meanwhile, in small bowl combine soup, water, vinegar, brown sugar, Worcestershire and pepper sauce. Spoon soup mixture over chops.

◆ Bake 15 minutes or until chops are no longer pink. Stir sauce before serving.

Makes 6 servings.

HAM IN PASTRY

1 CURE/81® Half Ham
1 (10 oz.) jar orange
  marmalade
3 (10 oz.) boxes single pie
  crust mix
1 egg, beaten

◆ Put ham in shallow roasting pan. Add 1 cup
water; cover pan with foil. Place in cold oven; set at
325° and heat 30 minutes. Remove from oven;
pour off water. Cool slightly; spread thickly with
marmalade.

◆ Prepare pie crust. Roll out in long rectangle,
⅜ inch thick. Place ham on one side of dough. Fold
remaining pastry over ham; trim. Seal edges well.

◆ Cover seams and decorate with festive shapes
cut from trimmings; attach with beaten egg. Brush
entire crust with egg.

◆ Return ham to baking pan. Increase heat to
375°; bake 45 minutes. Cool 15 minutes; remove
with large spatula.

Serves 8 to 10.

Courtesy: Geo. A. Hormel & Company

PINEAPPLE HAM SALAD

1 medium fresh pineapple
3 cups diced cooked ham,
  turkey or chicken
1 (6.25 oz.) pkg. long-grain
  and wild rice mix,
  prepared according to
  package directions
¾ cup chopped celery
2 tablespoons chopped
  scallions
⅛ cup vegetable oil
¼ cup red or white wine
  vinegar
2 tablespoons GREY
  POUPON® Dijon Mustard
¼ teaspoon ground ginger

◆ Cut pineapple in half lengthwise, slicing
through top, keeping the green leaves intact. Scoop
out pineapple; dice and set aside.

◆ In large, non-metal bowl, combine ham, cooked
rice, 1 cup diced pineapple (save remaining
pineapple for another use), celery and scallions; set
aside.

◆ In small bowl, using wire whisk, beat oil,
vinegar, mustard and ginger until smooth. Stir into
ham mixture until well coated.

◆ Cover and chill several hours to blend flavors.
Mound in pineapple halves and serve.

Ham In Pastry

PORK TENDERLOIN WITH RASPBERRY SAUCE SUPREME

1 lb. (approx.) pork
  tenderloin, cut into 8
  crosswise pieces
Cayenne pepper to taste
2 teaspoons butter
6 tablespoons red
  raspberry preserves
2 tablespoons red wine
  vinegar
1 tablespoon ketchup
½ teaspoon horseradish
½ teaspoon soy sauce
1 clove garlic, minced
2 kiwi fruit, peeled and
  thinly sliced
Fresh raspberries for
  garnish (optional)

◆ With flat side of wide knife press each pork tenderloin slice to 1-inch thickness. Lightly sprinkle both sides of each slice with cayenne pepper.

◆ Heat butter in nonstick skillet over medium-high heat. Add pork slices; cook 3 to 4 minutes each side.

◆ Meanwhile in small saucepan combine preserves, vinegar, ketchup, horseradish, soy sauce and garlic; simmer over low heat about 3 minutes, stirring occasionally. Keep warm.

◆ Place cooked pork on warm serving plate. Spoon sauce over. Garnish serving plate with kiwi slices and, if desired, fresh raspberries.

Makes 4 servings.

Courtesy: National Pork Producers Council

Garden Pork Sauté

2 tablespoons margarine or
butter, divided
1 (1 lb.) pork tenderloin,
cut into ½-inch-thick
slices, or 4 boneless pork
chops, ¾ inch thick
(about 1 lb.)
1 cup broccoli florets
1 large carrot, trimmed,
scraped and thinly sliced
(about ½ cup)
1 cup sliced mushrooms
(about 3 oz.)
1 (10¾ oz.) can
CAMPBELL'S® condensed
cream of broccoli soup
⅓ cup milk
3 slices bacon, cooked crisp
and crumbled (optional)
⅛ teaspoon pepper

◆ In 10-inch skillet over medium-high heat, in
1 tablespoon hot margarine, cook pork 10 minutes
or until browned on both sides. Remove; keep
warm.

◆ In same skillet over medium heat, in remaining
hot margarine, cook broccoli, carrot and mushrooms until tender and liquid is evaporated, stirring often.

◆ In small bowl combine soup, milk, bacon and
pepper; pour over vegetables. Heat to boiling.

◆ Return pork to skillet. Reduce heat to low.
Cover; cook 5 minutes or until pork is tender and
no longer pink, stirring occasionally.

Makes 4 servings.

PORK CHOPS IN PEACH SAUCE

10 pork chops, ½ inch thick
1¼ teaspoons salt
½ teaspoon allspice
¼ teaspoon pepper
3 tablespoons vegetable oil
1 (16 oz.) can DEL MONTE®
  Yellow Cling Sliced
  Peaches, drained,
  reserving ½ cup syrup
½ cup apricot preserves
1 teaspoon grated orange
  peel
2 cloves garlic, minced

◆ Season meat with salt, allspice and pepper. In large skillet brown meat on both sides in oil. Place meat in 13 x 9 x 2-inch baking dish.

◆ In blender container combine remaining ingredients including reserved syrup. Cover and blend until smooth. Pour over meat.

◆ Heat oven to 350°. Bake uncovered until meat is tender, about 40 to 45 minutes, basting occasionally.

◆ Remove meat to serving platter; spoon ½ cup sauce over meat. Serve with remaining sauce and garnish with parsley, if desired.

Makes 10 servings.

SUPER SAUSAGE & PEPPERS

4 red or green sweet bell
  peppers, sliced into thin
  strips
2 cloves garlic, minced
3 tablespoons vegetable oil
1½ lbs. sweet Italian
  sausage, sliced into
  1-inch pieces
1 (30 oz.) jar RAGÚ Chunky
  Gardenstyle —SUPER
  MUSHROOM
¾ pkg. (16-oz. size) rotelle,
  cooked and drained
¼ cup grated Parmesan
  cheese
2 cups (16 oz.) shredded
  mozzarella cheese

◆ In large skillet sauté peppers and garlic in hot oil until peppers are tender. Remove and set aside. To same skillet add sausage; brown thoroughly. Drain fat.

◆ In large bowl combine sausage, sautéed peppers, pasta sauce and rotelle.

◆ Heat oven to 350°. Spoon sausage mixture into 13 x 9-inch baking dish or casserole. Sprinkle with Parmesan and mozzarella cheeses.

◆ Cover and bake 40 minutes. Remove cover during last 15 minutes.

Serves 6 to 8.

Pork Chops in Peach Sauce

GRILLED PORK ROAST WITH PEPPER JELLY GLAZE

4 lb. pork loin roast, rolled and tied

FOR MARINADE:
1 cup *each* apple juice, cider vinegar and hot pepper jelly

FOR GLAZE:
¾ cup pepper jelly
¼ cup cider vinegar

◆ Place pork in large zip-lock bag. Heat marinade ingredients together until jelly melts; cool slightly; pour over pork. Seal bag. Refrigerate 12 to 24 hours.

◆ Prepare covered grill with banked coals. Remove pork from marinade, reserving marinade; insert thermometer in center of roast.

◆ When coals are hot place pork over drip pan; cover grill. Grill 1¼ hours or until thermometer reads 150°, basting occasionally with marinade.

(continued)

◆ Combine glaze ingredients; coat roast with glaze for last 10 minutes of grilling, bringing roast to internal temperature of 160°.

◆ Let rest 10 to 15 minutes before removing string and slicing.

Serves 16.

Courtesy: National Pork Producers Council

HARVEST PORK ROAST

1 (3½ to 4 lb.) boneless pork shoulder roast, netted or tied (Boston butt)
2 tablespoons vegetable oil
1 (10¾ oz.) can CAMPBELL'S® condensed cream of mushroom soup
1 pouch CAMPBELL'S® dry onion quality soup and recipe mix
1 teaspoon dried thyme leaves, crushed
1 bay leaf
1¼ cups water, divided
8 medium potatoes, quartered
8 medium carrots, scraped and cut into 2-inch pieces
2 tablespoons all-purpose flour

◆ In oven-safe, 5-quart Dutch oven over medium-high heat cook roast in hot oil until browned on all sides. Remove; set aside. Spoon off fat.

◆ Heat oven to 350°. In same Dutch oven combine soups, thyme, bay leaf and 1 cup water. Heat to boiling, stirring occasionally. Return roast to Dutch oven. Cover; bake 45 minutes.

◆ Turn roast; add potatoes and carrots. Cover; cook 1 hour 45 minutes or until roast and vegetables are fork-tender (170° internal temperature).

◆ Transfer roast and vegetables to platter. Remove netting or string from roast.

◆ In cup stir together flour and remaining water until smooth.

◆ In Dutch oven over medium heat, heat soup mixture to boiling. Gradually stir in flour mixture. Cook until mixture boils and thickens, stirring constantly (thin with additional water if necessary). Remove bay leaf before serving. Serve gravy with roast.

Makes 8 servings.

Country Pork With Beans (top), Three Bean Chili

THREE BEAN CHILI

½ lb. chorizo or other spicy
  cooked sausage, sliced
1 onion, chopped
2 cloves garlic, crushed
1 (14½ oz.) can DEL
  MONTE® Chili Style
  Chunky Tomatoes
1 (15 oz.) can barbecue-
  style beans
1 (15 oz.) can black or pinto
  beans, drained
1 (8¾ oz.) can kidney
  beans, drained

◆ In large saucepan cook sausage, onion and garlic until tender; drain. Add tomatoes and beans. Cover and simmer 15 minutes or until heated through, stirring occasionally.

◆ Garnish with sour cream and sliced green onion, if desired.

Makes 6 servings.

COUNTRY PORK WITH BEANS

2 slices bacon, diced
3 boneless pork chops
  (¾ lb.), sliced ¼ inch thick
  and trimmed of fat
1 medium onion, chopped
1 clove garlic, minced
1 teaspoon thyme, crushed
1 (17 oz.) can DEL MONTE®
  Green Lima Beans,
  drained
1 (14½ oz.) can DEL
  MONTE® Original Style
  Stewed Tomatoes,
  chopped
1 (8 oz.) can kidney beans,
  drained

◆ In large skillet, over low heat, cook bacon until just crisp.

◆ Raise heat to medium; stir in meat, onion, garlic and thyme.

◆ Stir fry for 5 minutes; drain off excess fat. Add remaining ingredients; bring to boil. Reduce heat and simmer, uncovered, 10 minutes.

◆ Season to taste with salt and pepper, if desired.

Makes 4 servings.

*J*AMBALAYA

6 oz. hot smoked sausage, sliced
2 (14½ oz.) cans DEL MONTE® Cajun Style Stewed Tomatoes
8 oz. medium shrimp, shelled and deveined, or 6 oz. ham, diced
1 cup uncooked rice
1 large clove garlic, minced
1 bay leaf
1 tablespoon chopped parsley

◆ In heavy 4-quart pot brown sausage (and ham if using) over low heat.

◆ Drain tomatoes reserving liquid. Add water to reserved liquid to measure 1½ cups.

◆ Add to sausage with tomatoes, shrimp (if using) and remaining ingredients. Bring to a boil. Stir; reduce heat to low.

◆ Cover; simmer 30 to 35 minutes or until liquid is absorbed, stirring occasionally. Remove bay leaf.

Makes 4 to 6 servings.

Adobe Pork Loin

3 cloves garlic, minced
1 teaspoon ground cloves
1 teaspoon ground
    coriander
1 teaspoon cumin
1 teaspoon coarsely
    ground black pepper
2½ lbs. boneless pork loin
1 (15 oz.) can HORMEL Chili
    No Beans
1½ cups water
3 medium onions, cut into
    1-inch pieces
Thin strips of lemon peel

◆ Heat oven to 350°. In small bowl combine garlic, cloves, coriander, cumin and pepper. Rub mixture on pork loin.

◆ In roasting pan combine chili and water. Place pork loin on chili mixture. Place onions around roast.

◆ Cover; bake 1 hour. Uncover and baste. Continue baking, basting occasionally, 1 hour or until meat thermometer inserted near center reaches 165°F.

◆ Serve sliced pork with chili and onions. Garnish with lemon peel.

Serves 4.

Lamb Chops With Zucchini and Peppers

LAMB CHOPS WITH ZUCCHINI AND PEPPERS

1 tablespoon olive oil

8 lamb chops, 1 inch thick, trimmed of excess fat

1 medium zucchini, trimmed and cut diagonally into ¼-inch-thick slices (about 1½ cups)

1 *each* red and yellow bell pepper, trimmed, seeded and cut into ½-inch-wide slices

1 clove garlic, minced

½ teaspoon dried oregano, crumbled

Salt and freshly ground pepper

◆ In large, heavy skillet heat oil over medium-high heat. Add lamb and sauté for 5 minutes on each side for rare, or longer to desired doneness. Remove to serving dish and keep warm.

◆ Reduce heat to medium; add zucchini, peppers, garlic and oregano. Toss to coat; cook 5 to 7 minutes or until crisp-tender, tossing frequently.

◆ Season with salt and pepper. Arrange vegetables around lamb; serve immediately.

Serves 4.

JAMAICAN FRUIT LAMB CHOPS

8 medium loin lamb chops, trimmed

1 (16 oz.) can DEL MONTE® Lite Sliced Peaches or Apricot Halves

2 teaspoons instant coffee crystals

2 tablespoons chopped parsley

Dash pepper

◆ In large skillet brown meat; remove and keep warm.

◆ Drain fruit, reserving liquid in skillet. Add coffee crystals. Cook over high heat 5 minutes to reduce and thicken liquid.

◆ Return meat to skillet; simmer 8 to 10 minutes, turning frequently.

◆ Add fruit, parsley and pepper. Cover, heat through, about 5 minutes, and serve.

Makes 4 servings.

HEARTY CHICKEN BAKE

3 cups hot mashed
potatoes
1 cup shredded Cheddar
cheese, divided
1 (2.8 oz.) can DURKEE
French Fried Onions,
divided
1½ cups cubed cooked
chicken
1 (10 oz.) pkg. frozen
mixed vegetables,
thawed and drained
1 (10¾ oz.) can condensed
cream of chicken soup
¼ cup milk
½ teaspoon DURKEE
Ground Mustard
¼ teaspoon DURKEE Garlic
Powder
¼ teaspoon DURKEE
Ground Black Pepper

◆ Heat oven to 350°. In medium bowl combine potatoes, half the cheese and half the onions; mix thoroughly. Spoon into greased, 1½-quart casserole spreading across bottom and up sides to form a shell.

◆ In large bowl combine chicken, mixed vegetables, soup, milk and seasonings; pour into potato shell.

◆ Bake uncovered, 30 minutes or until heated through. Top with remaining cheese and onions; bake, uncovered, 3 minutes or until onions are golden brown. Let stand 5 minutes before serving.

Makes 4 to 6 servings.

GARDEN CHICKEN STIR FRY

1 tablespoon oil
1 lb. boneless chicken
  breasts, cut into strips
⅔ cup diagonally sliced
  carrots
½ cup broccoli florets
1 medium onion, sliced
2 envs. LIPTON Cream of
  Chicken Flavor Cup-a-
  Soup Instant Soup
1 cup water
Salt and pepper to taste
Hot cooked rice or noodles

◆ In large skillet heat oil and cook chicken with vegetables over medium-high heat, stirring constantly, 5 minutes or until chicken is golden and vegetables are crisp-tender.

◆ Blend soup with water; add to skillet. Bring to a boil, then simmer, uncovered, stirring occasionally, 5 minutes or until sauce is thickened. Add salt and pepper. Serve over hot rice or noodles.

Serves 3.

CHICKEN TERIYAKI PITA POCKETS

6 boneless, skinless chicken
  breasts, split (approx. 2
  lbs.)
1 cup LAWRY'S Teriyaki
  Marinade with Pineapple
  Juice
1 tablespoon margarine or
  butter
1 medium onion, thinly
  sliced
1 cup reduced calorie
  mayonnaise
¼ cup finely chopped
  green onion
6 pita pockets
1 small head lettuce
2 medium tomatoes, sliced

◆ Place chicken breasts and marinade in resealable plastic bag. Seal bag and marinate 2 hours; drain and discard marinade.

◆ Prepare outdoor grill or broiler. Grill or broil chicken breasts 7 minutes on each side. Thinly slice and set aside.

◆ In small skillet over medium heat melt margarine. Sauté onion until tender; set aside.

◆ In small bowl combine mayonnaise and green onion.

◆ Cut top off pita breads and open to form pocket. Spread inside of each pocket with mayonnaise mixture. Place one lettuce leaf, one tomato slice, some onion and chicken slices in each pocket.

Serves 6.

CHICKEN TOSTADAS

12 OLD EL PASO® Tostada
  Shells
1 lb. boneless chicken
  breasts, cut into thin
  strips
¼ cup chopped onion
2 tablespoons butter
1 (16 oz.) jar OLD EL PASO®
  Thick 'n Chunky Salsa
1 (1¼ oz.) pkg. OLD EL
  PASO® Taco Seasoning
  Mix
1 (16 oz.) can OLD EL
  PASO® Refried Beans,
  heated
3 cups shredded lettuce
3 medium tomatoes,
  chopped
3 cups shredded Cheddar
  cheese (about 8 oz.)
Fresh coriander (optional)

◆ Heat tostada shells according to package directions. In medium skillet quickly cook chicken strips and onion in butter until chicken is browned.

◆ Add salsa and seasoning mix, reduce heat and simmer, uncovered, 10 minutes.

◆ To assemble, spread 1 heaping tablespoon refried beans on each shell. Spoon on approximately ⅓ cup chicken mixture. Top with lettuce, tomatoes and cheese. Garnish with coriander.

Makes 12 tostadas.

Place tostada shells on a baking sheet and heat according to package directions.

Cut chicken breasts into thin strips.

Spoon chicken mixture over refried beans. Top with lettuce, tomatoes and cheese.

TEX-MEX CHICKEN FAJITAS

1½ lbs. boneless, skinless chicken breasts, cut into 1½ x 3-inch strips
½ cup LAWRY'S Mesquite Marinade with Lime Juice
2 tablespoons salad oil
1 onion, sliced
1 green bell pepper, sliced
¾ teaspoon LAWRY'S Garlic Powder with Parsley

◆ In large bowl or resealable plastic bag combine chicken and marinade. Marinate 1 hour; drain and discard marinade.

◆ In large skillet heat oil; sauté onion, bell pepper, garlic powder and hot pepper sauce 8 minutes until crisp-tender. Set aside.

◆ In same skillet sauté chicken 8 to 10 minutes until no longer pink. Stir in vegetable mixture and tomato; heat through.

(continued)

½ teaspoon hot pepper
  sauce
1 tomato, cut into wedges
8 flour tortillas
2 tablespoons chopped
  cilantro for garnish
1 lime, cut into wedges

◆ Meanwhile, warm tortillas in oven 5 minutes. Remove; wrap in small towel to keep them soft.

◆ To serve, line serving platter with lettuce leaves. Scoop chicken mixture into center and top with cilantro. Arrange lime wedges around edge.

Makes 4 servings.

GRILLED TEX-MEX CHICKEN

½ cup sour cream
1 env. LIPTON Onion Recipe
  Soup Mix
2 tablespoons milk
1 tablespoon ground cumin
1 teaspoon chili powder
½ teaspoon thyme leaves
½ teaspoon oregano
1 (2½ to 3 lb.) chicken, cut
  into serving pieces

◆ Heat broiler or grill. In small bowl thoroughly combine all ingredients except chicken.

◆ Grill or broil chicken, turning and basting frequently with sour cream mixture, until chicken is done.

Makes about 4 servings.

Everyday Broccoli Cheese Chicken

1 tablespoon margarine or
butter
4 skinless, boneless chicken
breast halves (about
1 lb.)
1 (10¾ oz.) can
CAMPBELL'S® condensed
broccoli cheese soup
⅓ cup water or milk
2 cups broccoli florets
⅛ teaspoon pepper

◆ In 10-inch skillet heat margarine over medium heat; cook chicken 10 minutes or until browned on both sides. Spoon off fat.

◆ Stir in remaining ingredients. Heat to boiling. Reduce heat to low. Cover; simmer 10 minutes or until chicken is fork-tender and broccoli is done, stirring occasionally.

Makes 4 servings.

Skillet Herb-Roasted Chicken

2 tablespoons all-purpose
flour
¼ teaspoon ground sage
¼ teaspoon dried thyme
leaves, crushed
4 skinless, boneless chicken
breast halves, or 8
skinless, boneless chicken
thighs (about 1 lb.)
2 tablespoons margarine or
butter
1 (10¾ oz.) can
CAMPBELL'S® condensed
cream of chicken soup
½ cup water
Hot cooked rice or noodles

◆ On wax paper, combine flour, sage and thyme. Coat chicken lightly with flour mixture.

◆ In 10-inch skillet over medium-high heat, in hot margarine, cook chicken 15 minutes or until browned on both sides and no longer pink. Remove; set aside. Keep warm. Spoon off fat.

◆ In same skillet, combine soup and water; heat to boiling. Reduce heat to low. Cover; cook 5 minutes, stirring occasionally.

◆ Arrange chicken over rice. Spoon sauce over chicken.

Serves 4.

Everyday Broccoli Cheese Chicken (top), Skillet Herb-Roasted Chicken

CHICKEN AND CRISP VEGETABLE TOSS

1 (7 oz.) pkg. CREAMETTE®
Elbow Macaroni (2 cups
uncooked)

½ cup olive or vegetable
oil

2 tablespoons red wine
vinegar

2 tablespoons fresh lemon
juice

½ teaspoon tarragon leaves

¼ teaspoon dry mustard

¼ teaspoon pepper

2 cups sliced fresh
mushrooms

1 cup frozen green peas,
thawed

1 cup sliced pitted ripe
olives

1 small red bell pepper, cut
into small julienne strips

⅓ cup sliced green onions

2 tablespoons chopped
fresh parsley

2 (5 oz.) cans HORMEL®
Chunk Chicken, drained
and flaked

◆ Prepare macaroni according to package
directions; drain. In large skillet heat oil, vinegar,
lemon juice, tarragon, dry mustard and pepper.

◆ Add macaroni and remaining ingredients; toss
to coat. Heat through. Serve immediately.

Makes 6 to 8 servings.

Chicken à la Divan

3 cups cooked fresh broccoli spears, or 2 (10 oz.) pkgs. frozen broccoli spears, cooked and drained

1½ lbs. sliced cooked chicken breast, skinned and boned

¼ teaspoon rosemary

¼ teaspoon curry powder

3 tablespoons FLEISCHMANN'S® Regular or Sweet Unsalted Margarine

3 tablespoons all-purpose flour

1½ cups skim milk

6 tablespoons EGG BEATERS® 99% Real Egg Product

1 clove garlic, crushed

1 tablespoon lemon juice

Paprika

◆ Heat oven to 350°. In bottom of 2-quart, shallow baking dish or 6 individual baking dishes arrange broccoli.

◆ Place chicken slices over broccoli; sprinkle with rosemary and curry powder.

◆ Cover with foil and bake for 20 minutes or until hot.

◆ In saucepan melt margarine. Blend in flour. Cook over low heat, stirring, until smooth and bubbly.

◆ Remove from heat and gradually stir in milk. Return to heat and bring to a boil, stirring constantly.

◆ Gradually blend about ½ the hot mixture into Egg Beaters, then combine with remaining hot mixture. Stir in garlic and lemon juice.

◆ Spoon sauce over chicken and broccoli; sprinkle lightly with paprika and serve.

Makes 6 servings.

CREAM CHEESE &
SPINACH STUFFED CHICKEN ROLLS

6 boneless chicken breast
   halves
1 (8 oz.) pkg. cream cheese
½ cup chopped cooked
   spinach, drained
1 small clove garlic, minced
⅛ teaspoon nutmeg
Salt and freshly ground
   pepper to taste
1 large egg, beaten with
   1 tablespoon water
½ cup unseasoned dry
   bread crumbs
3 tablespoons butter,
   melted

◆ Heat oven to 375°. Flatten chicken between sheets of plastic wrap to uniform ¼-inch thickness.

◆ In large bowl beat cream cheese with next five ingredients until combined. Spoon equal amount of mixture across narrow end of each breast.

◆ Roll jellyroll style; secure with toothpicks. Dip in egg, then roll in crumbs; shake off excess.

◆ In baking dish arrange chicken in one layer, seam side down; drizzle with butter. Bake 25 to 30 minutes or until golden.

Serves 6.

Courtesy: National Dairy Board

Between two sheets of plastic wrap, flatten chicken to a uniform ¼-inch thickness.

Spoon cream cheese mixture across narrow end of chicken breast. Roll jellyroll style.

Secure rolls using toothpicks inserted at an angle.

GRILLED CHICKEN & PASTA SALAD

1 (16 oz.) pkg. bow tie
  pasta, cooked and
  drained
1 (12 oz.) jar marinated
  artichoke hearts, drained
1 (7 oz.) jar roasted red
  peppers, drained and
  sliced
⅓ cup slivered black olives
1 cup RAGÚ Chunky
  Gardenstyle—Super
  Vegetable Primavera
  Pasta Sauce
½ cup olive oil
2 tablespoons wine
  vinegar
2 tablespoons minced fresh
  parsley
½ teaspoon salt
1 lb. boneless, skinless
  chicken breasts
1 tablespoon toasted
  pignoli nuts

◆ In large bowl thoroughly combine first 9 ingredients. Cover and chill.

◆ Broil or grill chicken until thoroughly cooked. Thinly slice cooked chicken and serve warm over pasta salad. Garnish with pignoli nuts.

Serves 6 to 8.

GINGER CHICKEN ASPARAGUS

2 tablespoons vegetable
   oil, divided
1 lb. skinless, boneless
   chicken breasts, cut into
   1-inch pieces
¾ lb. fresh asparagus
   spears (12 to 15),
   trimmed and cut into
   1-inch pieces, or 1 (10 oz.)
   pkg. frozen asparagus
   cuts, thawed
2 medium carrots,
   diagonally sliced (about
   1 cup)
4 green onions, cut
   diagonally into 1-inch
   pieces (about 1 cup)
¼ teaspoon ground ginger
1 (10¾ oz.) can
   CAMPBELL'S® condensed
   cream of asparagus soup
¼ cup water
1 tablespoon soy sauce
Hot cooked rice

◆ In 10-inch skillet or wok over medium-high heat, in 1 tablespoon hot oil, stir-fry half the chicken until browned. Remove; set aside. Repeat with remaining chicken.

◆ In same skillet, in remaining 1 tablespoon oil, stir-fry asparagus, onions, carrots and ginger 3 minutes or until tender-crisp.

◆ Stir in soup, water and soy. Heat to boiling. Stir in reserved chicken. Reduce heat to low.

◆ Heat through, stirring occasionally. Serve over rice with additional soy, if desired.

Serves 4.

CHICKEN PRIMAVERA

1 tablespoon oil
¾ lb. boneless, skinless chicken breasts, cut into strips
1 small onion, chopped
1 cup broccoli florets
1 cup frozen green peas, thawed
1 carrot, cut into julienne strips
1 (13¾ oz.) can chicken broth
½ teaspoon dried basil leaves
Dash pepper
1½ cups MINUTE® Instant Brown Rice
⅓ cup grated Parmesan cheese

◆ In large skillet over medium-high heat cook and stir chicken in hot oil until browned.

◆ Add onion, broccoli, peas and carrot; cook and stir until vegetables are crisp-tender.

◆ Add broth, basil and pepper; bring to a boil. Stir in rice. Return to boil. Reduce heat; cover and simmer 5 minutes. Stir in cheese.

◆ Remove from heat; cover and let stand for 5 minutes.

Makes 4 servings.

CHICKEN PIZZARELLA

1 tablespoon olive oil
2 tablespoons onion, finely chopped
1 cup mushrooms, thickly sliced
1 small clove garlic, minced
½ teaspoon oregano
1 (8 oz.) can tomato sauce
Pepper to taste
8 chicken breast halves, boneless and skins removed
1 cup mozzarella cheese

◆ Heat oven to 350°. In small saucepan heat oil; add onion, mushrooms, garlic and oregano.

◆ Cook over low heat, stirring occasionally, until onion is soft. Stir in tomato sauce and pepper.

◆ Place chicken in 2-quart baking dish. Cover with sauce and bake, uncovered, 35 minutes.

◆ Put mozzarella on top and continue baking 5 more minutes or until cheese is bubbling. Serve over linguini.

Serves 8.

Courtesy: National Dairy Board

COUNTRY-STYLE CHICKEN AND HAM

1 sheet PEPPERIDGE FARM®
Frozen Puff Pastry

1 tablespoon margarine or
butter

1 medium onion, chopped
(about ½ cup)

½ cup cubed, cooked ham

1 (10¾ oz.) can
CAMPBELL'S® condensed
cream of chicken soup

1 (10 oz.) pkg. frozen
succotash (2 cups)

1 (8 oz.) can stewed
tomatoes, cut up

1 cup cubed cooked
chicken

1 teaspoon hot pepper
sauce

◆ Thaw pastry according to package directions. Heat oven to 400°.

◆ Meanwhile, in 2-quart saucepan over medium heat, in hot margarine, cook onion and ham until onion is tender and ham is browned, stirring often. Stir in soup, succotash, tomatoes, chicken and hot pepper sauce. Heat to boiling. Reduce heat to low. Cover; cook 20 minutes or until vegetables are tender, stirring occasionally.

◆ Cut pastry into desired shapes with cookie cutters. Place on baking sheet. Bake 20 minutes or until pastry is golden.

◆ Spoon chicken mixture into bowls. Top with pastry.

Serves 4.

COOL GRILLED CHICKEN SALAD

1½ lbs. boneless chicken breast, skinned and rinsed

1 cup LAWRY'S Mesquite Marinade with Lime Juice

¾ teaspoon LAWRY'S Garlic Salt

1 qt. mixed salad greens (a combination of three of the following: green leaf lettuce, Boston lettuce, arugula, Belgian endive and radicchio)

6 medium red new potatoes, cooked and cut into chunks

1 cup shredded carrots

Fresh salsa or salad dressing

Tortilla chips

◆ Place chicken in resealable plastic bag. Combine marinade and garlic salt; pour over chicken. Seal bag and refrigerate 30 or 40 minutes (or overnight).

◆ Prepare grill. Remove chicken from marinade; set marinade aside. Grill 5 to 7 minutes per side until golden. Baste with reserved marinade.

◆ Cool chicken and cut into strips. Cover and refrigerate.

◆ When ready to serve, arrange lettuce in shallow serving dish. Layer potatoes, carrots and chicken over lettuce; drizzle with salsa or dressing. Serve with tortilla chips.

Makes 4 servings.

CIDER MILL CHICKEN WITH APPLES

½ cup (1 stick) I CAN'T BELIEVE IT'S NOT BUTTER!®

2 tart cooking apples, peeled, cored and thickly sliced

1 teaspoon apple pie spice or ½ teaspoon *each* cinnamon and nutmeg

6 boneless, skinless chicken breast halves

1 teaspoon lemon pepper

1 teaspoon curry powder

½ cup apple cider

2 tablespoons apple cider vinegar

¼ cup golden raisins

½ cup plain non-fat yogurt

◆ In large skillet melt I Can't Believe It's Not Butter! over medium-high heat. Add apples in one layer and sprinkle with apple pie spice. Sauté until tender, stirring occasionally. Remove with a slotted spoon.

◆ Add chicken breasts in one layer. Sprinkle with lemon pepper and curry powder. Sauté, turning often, until chicken just begins to brown. Add apple cider, vinegar and raisins. Bring to a boil, reduce heat to low, cover and simmer for 10 minutes.

◆ With slotted spoon remove chicken from skillet and arrange with apples on serving platter. Keep warm.

◆ Remove skillet from heat and let cool for a minute. Beat in yogurt until smooth. (This will help avoid curdling.) Pour over chicken and apples.

Serves 6.

Use a melon baller or corer to evenly core apples before slicing.

Remove chicken from skillet using slotted spoon. Arrange on serving platter with apples.

Before adding yogurt, remove skillet from heat and let mixture cool. This will help prevent curdling.

SENSATIONAL TURKEY STROGANOFF

2 tablespoons margarine or
butter, divided
1 lb. boneless turkey
cutlets, cut into strips
1 medium onion, chopped
(about ½ cup)
1 (10¾ oz.) can
CAMPBELL'S® condensed
cream of mushroom soup
½ cup sour cream or plain
yogurt
½ teaspoon paprika
Hot cooked noodles
Chopped fresh parsley for
garnish

◆ In 10-inch skillet over medium-high heat, melt 1 tablespoon margarine. Add half of the turkey and half of the onion; cook until turkey is no longer pink and onion is tender, stirring often. Remove; set aside

◆ Repeat with remaining margarine, turkey and onion.

◆ In same skillet combine soup, sour cream and paprika. Return turkey mixture to skillet. Reduce heat to low. Heat through, stirring occasionally. Serve over noodles. Garnish with parsley.

Makes 4 servings.

TURKEY TETRAZZINI

1 (10¾ oz.) can
CAMPBELL'S® condensed
cream of mushroom soup
½ cup water
½ cup grated Parmesan
cheese
2 cups (about 4 oz. dry)
cooked spaghetti
1½ cups diced cooked
turkey or chicken
2 tablespoons chopped
fresh parsley or 1
teaspoon dried parsley
flakes
2 tablespoons chopped
pimiento (optional)

◆ In 2-quart saucepan over medium heat combine soup, water and cheese. Heat to boiling, stirring occasionally.

◆ Stir in spaghetti, turkey, parsley and pimiento. Heat through, stirring occasionally.

Makes 4 cups or 4 servings.

Turkey Tetrazini

POLYNESIAN CHICKEN

1 lb. skinless, boneless
chicken breasts
2 tablespoons butter or
margarine
1 medium green pepper,
cut into 1-inch pieces
¼ teaspoon salt
Dash pepper
2 (8 oz.) cans pineapple
chunks, liquid reserved
½ cup plus 2½ tablespoons
water, divided
⅓ cup HEINZ Apple Cider
Vinegar
2 tablespoons brown sugar
2 tablespoons soy sauce
1 teaspoon ginger
2½ tablespoons cornstarch
Hot buttered rice
Toasted slivered almonds

◆ Cut chicken into 2-inch strips. In large skillet melt butter, then sauté chicken and green pepper just until chicken changes color. Season with the salt and pepper. Stir in pineapple, pineapple liquid, ½ cup of the water and the next 4 ingredients. Cover; simmer 10 to 12 minutes or until chicken is cooked.

◆ Combine cornstarch and the remaining 2½ tablespoons water; stir into chicken mixture. Cook until sauce is thickened, stirring constantly. Serve over rice; garnish with almonds.

Serves 4.

CHINESE-STYLE SKEWERED CHICKEN

1 (8 oz.) can HUNT'S®
   Tomato Sauce
¼ cup packed light brown
   sugar
¼ cup LA CHOY® soy sauce
1 tablespoon minced
   ginger root
1 teaspoon minced garlic
2 lbs. chicken breast or
   thigh fillets, skinned and
   cut into 1-inch cubes
8 (10-inch) bamboo
   skewers
2 medium green peppers,
   cubed
2 medium onions, cubed
1 tablespoon olive oil
Hot cooked rice

◆ In bowl mix tomato sauce, sugar, soy sauce, ginger and garlic. Stir in chicken; cover and refrigerate 2 to 8 hours.

◆ Heat broiler. Skewer chicken and broil 7 to 10 minutes or until lightly browned. Turn and broil 7 minutes longer or to desired doneness.

◆ Meanwhile, in medium skillet sauté peppers and onions in olive oil for 5 minutes.

◆ Serve chicken and vegetables over rice.

Makes 4 servings.

Apricot-Dijon Glazed Chicken

Apricot-Dijon Glazed Chicken

¼ cup GREY POUPON®
   Dijon Mustard
2 tablespoons apricot
   preserves, melted
½ teaspoon grated fresh
   ginger
1 lb. chicken parts

◆ Heat grill or broiler. In small bowl combine mustard, apricot preserves and ginger.

◆ Grill chicken, turning and brushing frequently with glaze while cooking.

Makes 4 servings plus ⅓ cup glaze.

Festive Chicken Kabobs and Rice

1 teaspoon paprika
½ cup rice vinegar
2 tablespoons vegetable oil
1 teaspoon dried rosemary,
   crushed
2 cloves garlic, minced
1 lb. boneless, skinless
   chicken breasts, cut into
   1½-inch cubes
2 medium yellow squash,
   cut into ½-inch slices
1 medium zucchini, cut into
   ½-inch slices
1 large red, green or
   yellow bell pepper, cut
   into 1½-inch squares
1 (14¼ oz.) can chicken
   broth
1 cup UNCLE BEN'S®
   CONVERTED® Brand Rice
2 tablespoons chopped
   green onions

◆ In large bowl combine first five ingredients; mix well. Add chicken; marinate 30 minutes.

◆ Alternately thread chicken, yellow squash, zucchini and bell pepper onto skewers, reserving marinade.

◆ In medium saucepan combine broth, 1 tablespoon of marinade and rice. Bring to a boil. Cover; simmer 20 minutes. Stir in green onions; cover; let stand until liquid is absorbed, about 5 minutes.

◆ While rice is cooking, brush skewers with some of the reserved marinade. Broil 4 to 5 inches from heat 8 to 10 minutes, turning once during cooking and brushing with remaining marinade.

◆ Arrange kabobs over rice and serve.

Makes 6 servings.

SEAFOOD FLORENTINE BAKE

2 lbs. fish fillets (flounder, haddock or pollock)
1 teaspoon salt
½ teaspoon onion powder
½ teaspoon pepper
1 (10¾ oz. to 11 oz.) can condensed cream of shrimp or Cheddar cheese soup
1 (10 oz.) pkg. frozen chopped spinach, thawed and well drained
2 cups BISQUICK® baking mix
⅓ cup grated Parmesan cheese
1 cup milk
2 eggs

◆ Heat oven to 350°. Arrange fish fillets in a greased 13 x 9 x 2-inch baking dish; sprinkle with salt, onion powder and pepper. Spoon soup over fillets; top with spinach.

◆ Beat remaining ingredients with wire whisk or hand beater about 1 minute or until almost smooth; pour over spinach.

◆ Bake uncovered about 40 minutes or until top is golden brown. Let stand 10 minutes before serving.

Makes 8 servings.

DIJON SHRIMP SCAMPI

1 lb. large shrimp, cleaned
and deveined, or 1 lb.
boneless chicken breast,
cut into thin strips
1 clove garlic, minced
2 tablespoons BLUE
BONNET Margarine
⅓ cup GREY POUPON®
Country Dijon Mustard
¼ cup lemon juice
¼ cup parsley
Hot cooked rice (optional)

◆ In large skillet, over medium-high heat, cook and stir shrimp and garlic in margarine until just pink.

◆ Blend in mustard, lemon juice and parsley; heat through. Serve over rice, if desired.

Serves 4.

SHRIMP IN THE PINK

1 tablespoon olive or
  vegetable oil
1 tablespoon IMPERIAL
  Margarine
¼ teaspoon LAWRY'S
  Garlic Powder with
  Parsley
1 lb. medium shrimp,
  uncooked and cleaned
1¾ cups water
½ cup milk
1 pkg. LIPTON Noodles &
  Sauce—Tomato Herb
  Alfredo or Alfredo
¼ cup chopped green
  onions

◆ In large skillet heat oil, margarine and garlic powder and cook shrimp over medium-high heat, stirring constantly, until shrimp turns pink; remove and set aside. Add water and milk; bring to boiling.

◆ Stir in noodles and sauce; reduce heat and simmer, stirring occasionally, 8 minutes or until noodles are tender.

◆ Stir in shrimp and green onions; heat through.

Makes about 2 servings.

SALMON FILLETS BAKED IN A POUCH WITH ORIENTAL-STYLE VEGETABLES

5 tablespoons I CAN'T BELIEVE IT'S NOT BUTTER!®, melted

2 tablespoons soy sauce

4 salmon fillets (6 to 8 oz. each), or any firm fleshed fish such as tuna, swordfish or halibut

¼ lb. snow peas, trimmed

2 scallions, trimmed and thinly sliced

4 teaspoons chopped fresh ginger (optional)

Freshly ground pepper to taste

◆ Heat oven to 450°. In small bowl blend I Can't Believe It's Not Butter! and soy sauce together.

◆ Lay each fillet on bottom half of a 12-inch square of aluminum foil.

◆ Equally divide snow peas; arrange on top of each fillet. Repeat with scallions and ginger. Spoon sauce evenly over each; top with a grating of pepper to taste.

◆ Fold foil over fish, crimping edges to seal well. Place on cookie sheet and bake 15 minutes. Open carefully with tip of a knife and pull back foil. Transfer to warm plates.

Serves 4.

Top each salmon fillet with ¼ of the snow peas. Repeat with scallions and ginger. Spread sauce over each.

Fold foil over fish, crimping edges to seal well.

Open foil packages carefully using the tip of a knife. Pull back foil.

SPAGHETTI AND SHRIMP PLATTER

½ of a (1 lb.) pkg.
  CREAMETTE® Spaghetti,
  uncooked
3 tablespoons butter or
  margarine
3 tablespoons olive oil
½ lb. medium shrimp,
  shelled and deveined
1 clove garlic, minced
⅓ cup grated Parmesan
  cheese
¼ cup chopped fresh dill
1 teaspoon salt
½ teaspoon coarsely
  ground pepper

◆ Prepare spaghetti according to package directions; drain.

◆ In large skillet heat butter and olive oil. Add shrimp and garlic; cook and stir until shrimp are opaque.

◆ Combine hot cooked spaghetti, shrimp mixture, Parmesan cheese, dill, salt and pepper. Toss to mix.

◆ Arrange on warm serving platter. Serve immediately. Refrigerate leftovers.

Serves 4.

Scallops With Basil in Lemon Sauce

4 tablespoons I CAN'T
  BELIEVE IT'S NOT
  BUTTER!®
1 clove garlic, minced
1½ lbs. bay or sea scallops,
  rinsed and well dried
3 tablespoons chopped
  fresh basil leaves
2 tablespoons fresh lemon
  juice
Salt and freshly ground
  pepper to taste

◆ In large, heavy skillet, over medium heat, melt I Can't Believe It's Not Butter! Add garlic and cook until softened. Do not brown.

◆ Add scallops and basil and sauté over medium-high heat, stirring constantly, for 2 minutes.

◆ Add lemon juice and continue cooking, stirring constantly, 2 to 3 minutes longer. Season with salt and pepper. Serve immediately.

Serves 4.

Herb-Baked Fish and Rice

1½ cups hot chicken
  bouillon
½ cup uncooked regular
  rice
¼ teaspoon DURKEE Italian
  Seasoning
¼ teaspoon DURKEE Garlic
  Powder
1 (10 oz.) pkg. frozen
  chopped broccoli,
  thawed and drained
1 (2.8 oz.) can DURKEE
  French Fried Onions,
  divided
1 tablespoon grated
  Parmesan cheese
1 lb. unbreaded fish fillets,
  thawed if frozen
DURKEE Paprika (optional)
½ cup (2 oz.) shredded
  Cheddar cheese

◆ Heat oven to 375°. In 8 x 12-inch baking dish combine hot bouillon, uncooked rice and seasonings.

◆ Bake, covered, for 10 minutes. Top with broccoli, ½ can french fried onions and the Parmesan cheese. Place fish fillets diagonally down center of dish; sprinkle fish lightly with paprika, if used.

◆ Bake, covered, for 20 to 25 minutes or until fish flakes easily with fork.

◆ Loosen rice by carefully stirring with a fork. Top fish with Cheddar cheese and the remaining onions; bake, uncovered, for 3 minutes or until onions are golden brown.

TASTY TUNA TORTILLAS

⅓ cup WISH-BONE Healthy
 Sensation! French
 Dressing
¼ cup water
1 stalk celery, sliced
1 small onion, finely
 chopped
1 medium red or green
 pepper, chopped
1 (6½ oz.) can tuna packed
 in water, drained and
 flaked
1 (3¼ oz.) can tuna packed
 in water, drained and
 flaked
8 flour tortillas, warmed

ASSORTED TOPPERS:
Lite sour cream
Low fat plain yogurt
Low fat cottage cheese
Hot pepper sauce
Shredded lettuce
Shredded carrots
Bean sprouts
Alfalfa sprouts

◆ In 10-inch skillet bring French dressing, water, celery, onion and pepper to the boiling point. Reduce heat; simmer, stirring occasionally, 5 minutes.

◆ Stir in tuna; heat through. Spoon mixture in tortillas and roll up. Serve with assorted toppers.

Makes about 4 servings.

IMPOSSIBLE TUNA AND CHEDDAR PIE

2 cups chopped onions
¼ cup margarine or butter
2 (6½ oz.) cans solid white tuna in water, drained
2 cups shredded Cheddar cheese, divided (8 oz.)
3 eggs
1¼ cups milk
1 cup BISQUICK® baking mix
⅛ teaspoon pepper
2 tomatoes, thinly sliced

◆ Heat oven to 400°. Grease a 10 x 1½-inch glass pie plate, an 8 x 8 x 2-inch square baking dish or six 10-ounce custard cups.

◆ In 10-inch skillet cook onions and margarine over low heat, stirring occasionally, until onions are light brown.

◆ Sprinkle tuna, 1 cup of the cheese and the onions in the pie plate.

◆ Beat eggs, milk, baking mix and pepper in blender on high 15 seconds (or with hand beater or wire whisk 1 minute). Pour into pie plate or square dish.

(continued)

◆ Bake 25 to 30 minutes (custard cups 20 to 25 minutes) or until knife inserted in center comes out clean. Top with tomato slices and remaining cheese.

◆ Bake 3 to 5 minutes longer or until cheese is melted. Cool 5 minutes.

Makes 6 to 8 servings.

*S*TUFFED *F*LOUNDER *R*OLLS

3 large flounder fillets (about 1¼ lbs.)
Freshly ground pepper to taste
2 tablespoons olive oil
1½ cups sliced mushrooms
¼ cup minced onion
½ cup diced carrots, cooked tender-crisp
1 tablespoon minced parsley
½ cup HIDDEN VALLEY RANCH® Take Heart Italian Salad Dressing

◆ Heat oven to 400°. Cut fillets in half lengthwise. Sprinkle with pepper.

◆ Roll up each fillet lengthwise and place in greased muffin tins, leaving a cavity in the center.

◆ In skillet over medium-low heat sauté mushrooms and onion in oil until soft. Do not brown. Stir in carrots and parsley.

◆ Stuff mixture into fish cavities. Spoon dressing over fillets.

◆ Bake 15 minutes. Remove from tins and spoon juices over each fillet.

Serves 4 to 6.

Roll up each fillet lengthwise starting at the narrow end.

Place fillets in greased muffin tins, making sure to leave a cavity in the center.

Stuff mixture into cavity and spoon dressing over fillets.

GINGER SHRIMP AND SCALLOPS OVER RICE

1½ cups UNCLE BEN'S® Fast
   Cook CONVERTED® Brand
   Rice
2 tablespoons butter or
   margarine, divided
½ lb. medium or large
   shrimp, peeled and
   deveined
½ lb. sea or bay scallops
8 oz. snow peas (about
   2 cups)
1 cup chicken broth
2 teaspoons cornstarch
1 tablespoon shredded
   fresh ginger
¼ cup thinly sliced green
   onions with tops

◆ Cook rice according to package directions; keep warm in serving dish.

◆ While rice is cooking, in 10-inch skillet over medium-high heat, melt 1 tablespoon of the butter. Add shrimp and scallops to skillet. Cook and stir until cooked through, about 3 minutes. Remove to bowl; reserve.

◆ Melt remaining butter in same skillet. Add snow peas; cook and stir until crisp-tender, about 2 minutes. Add snow peas to bowl with shrimp and scallops.

◆ Combine broth and cornstarch; add to skillet with ginger. Cook and stir until very thick, about 1 minute.

◆ Return shrimp mixture to skillet; heat through. Stir in green onions; pour mixture over warm rice.

Makes 4 servings.

Sweet Red Pepper & Mushroom Quesadillas

1 medium red onion, finely chopped

1 lb. fresh mushrooms, sliced

1 clove garlic, minced

1 teaspoon oregano

2 tablespoons oil

1 (10¾ oz.) can CAMPBELL'S® condensed Italian tomato soup

8 flour tortillas

2 cups red bell peppers, seeded and finely sliced

2 cups grated Monterey Jack or Cheddar cheese

◆ Heat oven to 350°. In large skillet sauté onion, mushrooms, garlic and oregano in oil over medium heat until lightly browned, about 5 minutes.

◆ Stir in soup and heat thoroughly.

◆ Place 4 tortillas on lightly greased baking sheet and spoon soup mixture equally onto them. Top with equal amounts of pepper strips, cheese and remaining tortillas.

◆ Bake 10 minutes or until cheese is melted. Cut into quarters and serve immediately. If desired, serve with sour cream and salsa on the side.

Serves 4.

Sauté onion, mushrooms, garlic and oregano until lightly browned, approximately 5 mintues.

Top tortillas first with soup mixture, then equal amounts of pepper strips and cheese.

Cut tortillas into quarters and serve immediately.

Frittata Primavera

1 tablespoon
FLEISCHMANN'S®
Margarine
1 medium onion, chopped
1 medium red or green
pepper, cut into strips
1 medium potato, peeled
and grated (about 1 cup)
1 cup coarsely chopped
broccoli
1 teaspoon dried oregano
leaves
¼ teaspoon ground black
pepper
1 (8 oz.) container EGG
BEATERS® Cholesterol-
Free 99% Real Egg
Product

◆ In 10-inch nonstick omelet pan melt margarine over medium-low heat. Add onion, pepper, potato, broccoli, oregano and black pepper; cover and cook, stirring frequently, until vegetables are tender-crisp.

◆ With mixer at high speed beat Egg Beaters for 2 minutes until light and fluffy; pour over vegetables.

◆ Cover; cook over low heat 5 to 7 minutes until eggs are set. Serve from pan or carefully invert onto warm serving plate immediately.

Makes 4 servings.

Eggs 'n' Veggie Pita Sandwich

1 (7.5 oz.) container EGG
BEATERS® Vegetable
Omelette Mix
1 teaspoon
FLEISCHMANN'S®
Margarine
4 lettuce leaves
2 large whole wheat pita
pockets, halved

◆ Scramble omelette mix according to package directions using margarine.

◆ Serve hot in lettuce-lined pita pocket.

VARIATIONS:

◆ Add to omelette mix: ¼ teaspoon curry powder, ¼ teaspoon chili powder, ½ teaspoon dried tarragon or ½ teaspoon Italian seasoning.

◆ Top filled pita with drained, crushed pineapple, chopped avocado, alfalfa sprouts or chopped tomato.

Serves 4.

Meatless Chili

2 tablespoons MAZOLA
  corn oil
1½ cups chopped onions
3 cloves garlic, minced
2 tablespoons chili powder
½ teaspoon ground cumin
1 cup diced carrots
1 green pepper, chopped
2 (14½ to 16 oz.) cans
  tomatoes in juice,
  undrained
1 (16 oz.) can chick peas,
  drained
1 (15 oz.) can kidney beans,
  drained
1 (10 oz.) pkg. frozen corn,
  thawed
1 to 2 pickled jalapeño
  peppers, chopped
  (optional)

◆ In 5-quart saucepan heat corn oil over medium heat. Add onions, garlic, chili powder and cumin; sauté 5 minutes or until tender, stirring occasionally.

◆ Add carrots and green pepper; sauté 2 minutes.

◆ Add tomatoes with juice, crushing tomatoes with spoon. Stir in chick peas, kidney beans, corn and jalapeño peppers. Bring to boil.

◆ Reduce heat; cover and simmer 30 to 35 minutes, stirring occasionally. If desired, serve with rice.

Serves 8.

AUTUMN STUFFED SQUASH

**2 small acorn squash,
halved, seeded**

**4 tablespoons I CAN'T
BELIEVE IT'S NOT
BUTTER!®, divided**

**½ cup *each* diced onion,
carrots and red bell
pepper**

**½ cup *each* thickly sliced
zucchini and mushrooms**

1 small clove garlic, minced

◆ Heat oven to 350°. Melt 1 tablespoon I Can't Believe It's Not Butter! and brush on cut surfaces of squash. Place cut side down in a large baking dish without crowding. Add enough water to cover bottom of pan. Bake 30 minutes.

◆ In medium skillet melt remaining I Can't Believe It's Not Butter! over medium heat. Sauté remaining ingredients 5 minutes only, stirring frequently.

◆ Spoon vegetables into squash halves. Bake 20 to 25 minutes or until squash is tender.

Serves 4.

HERB-SPINACH-CHEESE TART

1 (9-inch) deep-dish frozen pie shell, thawed, or (9-inch) homemade pie shell

3 eggs

1½ cups lowfat milk

½ teaspoon Italian seasoning

¼ teaspoon salt

⅛ teaspoon ground black pepper

1 (9 oz.) pkg. frozen chopped spinach, thawed and excess liquid squeezed out

2 cups (8 oz.) shredded lowfat mozzarella cheese, divided

2 small tomatoes, sliced

◆ Heat oven to 450°. Pierce pie shell with fork. Bake until pale gold, about 8 minutes. Cool. Reduce oven to 350°.

◆ In medium bowl combine eggs, milk, Italian seasoning, salt and pepper. Add spinach and 1 cup of the mozzarella cheese to the egg mixture.

◆ Pour into cooled pie shell. Top with tomato slices. Sprinkle with remaining cheese.

◆ Bake until a knife inserted in the center comes out clean, about 50 minutes. Let stand 10 minutes before serving.

Serves 6.

Courtesy: National Dairy Board

PEPPERED PAN POTATOES

½ teaspoon salt
¼ teaspoon dried basil leaves
¼ teaspoon dried thyme leaves
¼ teaspoon ground pepper
6 tablespoons (18 teaspoons) I CAN'T BELIEVE IT'S NOT BUTTER!®, melted; divided
2 lbs. potatoes, peeled, very thinly sliced; divided
6 tablespoons finely chopped onion, divided

◆ Heat oven to 425°. In small bowl stir together salt, basil, thyme and pepper.

◆ Place 2 tablespoons of the melted I Can't Believe It's Not Butter! in 10-inch, non-stick skillet. (If handle is not ovenproof, wrap with foil.) Arrange ⅓ of the potato slices in a circular pattern in bottom of skillet. Sprinkle with about ¼ teaspoon of the seasonings, 4 teaspoons of the melted I Can't Believe It's Not Butter! and 2 tablespoons of the onion.

◆ Repeat layering potatoes, seasonings, melted I Can't Believe It's Not Butter! and onion two more times.

◆ Cover skillet with foil; press layers down. Secure foil to skillet and bake 20 minutes or until potatoes are tender.

◆ Remove from oven; press layers down with a spatula. Let stand 10 minutes. Invert onto serving platter to unmold potatoes. Remove from skillet and serve.

Serves 6 to 8.

Ranch Potato Salad Primavera

RANCH POTATO SALAD PRIMAVERA

4 cups red potatoes, diced,
   cooked and cooled
Salt and pepper to taste
1 cup cooked broccoli
   florets
1 small yellow zucchini,
   sliced
1 stalk celery, chopped
½ cup diced red pepper
2 green onions, chopped
1 (8 oz.) bottle WISH-BONE
   Healthy Sensation! Ranch
   Dressing

◆ In large bowl sprinkle potatoes with salt and pepper. Add remaining ingredients and marinate in refrigerator at least 2 hours.

◆ (Note: For a tasty pasta salad, substitute 4 cups pasta, cooked and cooled, for potatoes.)

Makes about 8 cups salad.

BROCCOLI CHEESE SCALLOPED POTATOES

2 tablespoons butter or
   margarine
1 small onion, sliced
1 (10¾ oz.) can
   CAMPBELL'S® condensed
   broccoli cheese soup
⅓ cup milk
⅛ teaspoon pepper
4 medium potatoes,
   cooked and sliced ¼ inch
   thick (about 3½ cups)
Chopped fresh parsley for
   garnish

◆ In 10-inch skillet heat margarine over medium heat; cook onion until tender.

◆ Add remaining ingredients except parsley. Heat to boiling. Reduce heat to low. Cover; simmer 5 minutes or until hot.

◆ Garnish with parsley.

Makes 4 servings.

AUTUMNAL WILD RICE PILAF

1 (10 oz.) pkg. white and
   wild rice mix
1 large golden apple,
   unpeeled, cored and
   diced
1 carrot, scraped and
   shredded
1 green onion (scallion),
   minced
¼ cup golden raisins
¼ cup minced parsley
¼ cup sliced almonds
¼ cup I CAN'T BELIEVE IT'S
   NOT BUTTER!®, melted
2 teaspoons poppy seeds
1 teaspoon grated lemon
   peel
½ teaspoon cinnamon
1 tablespoon apple juice

◆ In medium, covered saucepan cook rice according to directions on package.

◆ In large bowl place apple, carrot, onion, raisins, parsley and almonds. Add cooked rice; toss together.

◆ In small bowl combine I Can't Believe It's Not Butter! with remaining ingredients. Add to rice mixture and toss to combine.

Serves 6.

*R*ATATOUILLE *R*ICE

1 (Family Size) bag UNCLE BEN'S® Boil-In Bag CONVERTED® Brand Rice
1⅓ cups chopped onion
⅔ cup sliced yellow squash
⅔ cup sliced zucchini
½ cup coarsely chopped red or green pepper
2 cloves garlic, minced
2 teaspoons dried basil, crushed
½ teaspoon salt (optional)
1 large tomato, diced
1 tablespoon chopped parsley

◆ Cook rice according to package directions. In 10-inch, non-stick skillet cook onion, stirring constantly, 1 minute.

◆ Stir in remaining ingredients except tomato and parsley. Cover; cook over low heat, stirring occasionally, until vegetables are tender, about 10 minutes.

◆ Stir in tomato and rice. Cover; simmer 10 minutes, stirring occasionally.

◆ Sprinkle with parsley and serve.

Makes 4 servings.

CHEDDAR RICE AND SPINACH BAKE

1 egg
½ cup SHEDD'S® COUNTRY
  CROCK® Fresh Cheddar
  Spreadable Cheese
1 (10 oz.) pkg. frozen
  chopped spinach, thawed
  and drained
2 cups cooked rice
1 medium onion, chopped
  (about ½ cup)
¼ teaspoon nutmeg
½ teaspoon salt
Freshly ground pepper to
  taste
¼ cup SHEDD'S® SPREAD
  COUNTRY CROCK®,
  melted

◆ Heat oven to 350°. In medium bowl beat egg. Add cheese, by the spoonful, to the bowl. Do not blend.

◆ Add remaining ingredients and mix thoroughly.

◆ Coat 1½-quart baking dish with an additional tablespoon Shedd's Spread Country Crock. Spoon in mixture and smooth the top. Cover.

◆ Bake 20 minutes. Serve.

Serves 4 to 6.

BROWN RICE WITH BLACK BEANS

1 tablespoon oil
1 medium onion, chopped
1 (14½ oz.) can stewed
  tomatoes with their juice
1 (16 oz.) can black beans
  with their juice
1 teaspoon oregano leaves
½ teaspoon garlic powder,
  or 1 clove fresh garlic,
  crushed
1½ cups MINUTE® Instant
  Brown Rice

◆ In large, deep skillet heat oil and stir onion until tender but not browned.

◆ Add tomatoes, beans, oregano and garlic powder; bring to a boil.

◆ Stir in rice. Return to boil; cover, reduce heat and simmer 5 minutes.

◆ Remove from heat and let stand 5 minutes or until rice is tender

Makes 8 servings.

Parsley Ginger Carrots (top), Carrots Elegante

PARSLEY GINGER CARROTS

1 lb. young carrots,
  trimmed and peeled
1 cup water
2 tablespoons I CAN'T
  BELIEVE IT'S NOT
  BUTTER!®, melted
1 teaspoon sugar
½ teaspoon ground ginger
1 tablespoon flat leaf
  parsley, minced
1 tablespoon lemon juice

◆ Cut carrots lengthwise into quarters, then into 1-inch pieces.

◆ In small saucepan cook carrots in water until tender-crisp; drain.

◆ In small skillet combine I Can't Believe It's Not Butter!, sugar, ginger, parsley and lemon juice. Add carrots, tossing well to coat.

◆ Cook over low heat for 3 to 4 minutes. Toss again and serve.

Serves 4.

CARROTS ELEGANTE

1 lb. carrots, thinly sliced
¼ cup golden raisins
¼ cup I CAN'T BELIEVE IT'S
  NOT BUTTER!®
3 tablespoons honey
1 tablespoon lemon juice
¼ teaspoon ground ginger
¼ cup sliced, unpeeled
  almonds

◆ Heat oven to 375°. Cook carrots, covered, in ½ inch boiling water for 8 minutes; drain.

◆ Place carrots in 1-quart baking dish. Stir in raisins, I Can't Believe It's Not Butter!, honey, lemon juice and ginger.

◆ Bake, uncovered, for 35 minutes, stirring occasionally. Sprinkle with almonds before serving.

Serves 4.

STUFFED TOMATOES

8 medium tomatoes
1 (10 oz.) pkg. frozen
   chopped spinach, thawed
6 tablespoons SHEDD'S®
   SPREAD COUNTRY
   CROCK® (stick), divided
½ cup COUNTRY CROCK®
   Fresh Garden Vegetable
   Spreadable Cheese Snack
¾ cup fresh bread crumbs,
   divided
Salt and pepper to taste

◆ Slice ¼ inch off top of each tomato; discard. Using spoon, gently scoop out seeds and core; discard. Turn tomato shells upside down for 10 minutes to drain.

◆ In medium skillet melt 4 tablespoons Shedd's Spread Country Crock. Add spinach; sauté uncovered 7 minutes. Remove from heat. Stir in cheese; fold in ½ cup bread crumbs; set aside.

◆ Heat oven to 400°. Grease 13 x 9-inch baking dish with 1 tablespoon Shedd's Spread Country Crock. Lightly sprinkle inside of each tomato with salt and pepper; place upright in baking dish.

◆ Fill each tomato with cheese mixture, mounding slightly. Top with remaining bread crumbs and a dab of Shedd's Spread Country Crock. Bake 25 minutes. Serve immediately.

Serves 8.

LIGHT AND SAUCY VEGETABLE MEDLEY

1⅓ cups 1% milk
¾ lb. red potatoes, finely chopped
2 cloves garlic, pressed
¼ teaspoon salt
⅛ teaspoon pepper
2 cups (8 oz.) fresh chopped vegetables (such as broccoli, red peppers, onions and mushrooms)
¾ cup finely shredded Asiago or Parmesan cheese, divided

◆ In large saucepan slowly heat milk, potatoes, garlic, salt and pepper until small bubbles appear at edges of pan. Cook, stirring frequently, about 15 minutes or until tender.

◆ Mash just enough potatoes to thicken mixture. Stir in vegetables; heat through.

◆ Remove from heat; stir in ½ cup cheese. Top with remaining cheese. Serve immediately.

Serves 6.

Courtesy: National Dairy Board

ITALIAN BAKED EGGPLANT

2 eggplants (about 1¼ lbs. each), peeled and sliced into ¼-inch slices
Salt
2 cups Italian seasoned bread crumbs
1 cup grated Parmesan cheese, divided
3 eggs, beaten
2 tablespoons water
Canola oil as needed
1 (27½ oz.) jar RAGÚ Today's Recipe Pasta Sauce —Tomato & Herbs

◆ Layer eggplant slices on paper towels. Sprinkle lightly with salt; continue to layer using paper towels. Let drain about 40 minutes.

◆ In medium bowl combine bread crumbs with ½ cup Parmesan cheese.

◆ In another bowl combine eggs and water. Dip each eggplant slice into egg, then into bread crumb mixture.

◆ In large skillet brown eggplant in hot oil on both sides; drain well on paper towels.

◆ Spread evenly ½ cup pasta sauce in 13 x 9-inch baking dish. Layer half the eggplant slices, 1 cup pasta sauce and ¼ cup Parmesan cheese. Repeat layers. Cover with foil.

◆ Heat oven to 375°. Bake 45 minutes or until bubbly.

Serves 6.

Place eggplant slices on paper towels. Sprinkle lightly with salt. Drain for approximately 40 minutes.

Dip eggplant slices into egg, then into bread crumb mixture.

Brown eggplant in oil. Remove and drain well on paper towels.

Golden Corn and Broccoli (top), Green Beans With Fresh Dill and Scallions

GOLDEN CORN AND BROCCOLI

1 bunch (1½ lbs.) broccoli,
  cut up or 1 (20 oz.) pkg.
  frozen broccoli cuts
1 cup water
1 (10¾ oz.) can
  CAMPBELL'S® condensed
  golden corn soup
½ cup shredded Cheddar
  cheese (2 oz.)
¼ cup milk
Dash pepper

◆ In 3-quart saucepan combine broccoli and water. Over high heat, heat to boiling. Reduce heat to low. Cover; cook 8 minutes or until broccoli is tender-crisp, stirring occasionally. Drain in colander.

◆ In same saucepan combine soup, cheese, milk and pepper. Return broccoli to saucepan. Over medium heat, heat through, stirring occasionally.

Makes 5 cups or 8 servings.

GREEN BEANS WITH FRESH DILL AND SCALLIONS

3 qts. water
1 lb. fresh string beans,
  trimmed and halved
3 tablespoons I CAN'T
  BELIEVE IT'S NOT
  BUTTER!®
5 scallions (green onions),
  trimmed and thickly
  sliced
3 tablespoons fresh dill,
  finely chopped
Salt and freshly ground
  pepper to taste

◆ In large pot bring water to a boil. Add beans and cook over medium heat, covered, 7 minutes; drain.

◆ In large skillet, over medium heat, melt I Can't Believe It's Not Butter!; sauté scallions 3 to 5 minutes or until wilted.

◆ Add beans; toss with I Can't Believe It's Not Butter and scallions; cook 5 to 7 minutes or until tender.

◆ Add dill, salt and pepper; toss to completely coat beans.

Serves 4 to 6.

DILLY PEA SOUFFLÉ

1 (17 oz.) can DEL MONTE®
   Sweet Peas, drained and
   divided
¼ cup butter or margarine
¼ cup flour
1 cup milk
6 eggs, separated
¼ cup plus 1 tablespoon
   grated Parmesan cheese,
   divided
2 teaspoons Dijon mustard
½ teaspoon dill weed
⅛ teaspoon salt
½ teaspoon cream of tartar

◆ Heat oven to 375°. Reserve ⅓ cup peas; purée remaining peas in food processor or blender. Set aside.

◆ In medium saucepan melt butter over low heat. Blend in flour; slowly add milk. Cook, stirring constantly, until thickened. Cool to room temperature.

◆ Add egg yolks; mix well. Stir in all peas, ¼ cup cheese, mustard, dill weed and salt. Transfer to large bowl.

◆ In another large bowl beat egg whites until frothy. Add cream of tartar; beat until stiff, but not dry. Fold into pea mixture.

◆ Grease 1½-quart soufflé dish; dust with remaining Parmesan cheese. Make 2-inch foil collar around soufflé dish.

◆ Spoon mixture into dish; place in pan containing 1 inch hot water.

◆ Bake 45 to 50 minutes or until puffed and golden. Remove collar and serve immediately.

Serves 4 to 6.

GINGERED PEAS AND PEPPERS

1 tablespoon vegetable oil
½ cup julienne red or green
 pepper
½ cup chopped onion
½ teaspoon minced fresh
 ginger root or ¼
 teaspoon powdered
 ginger
1 (17 oz.) can DEL MONTE®
 Sweet Peas, drained
1 tablespoon toasted
 sesame seeds

◆ In saucepan heat oil; add pepper, onion and ginger. Cook over low heat until soft. Do not brown.

◆ Add peas and sesame seeds. Cover and heat through. Season to taste with salt and pepper.

Makes 4 servings.

COOL FRENCH BEAN SALAD

1 lb. green beans, trimmed
 and cut into thin julienne
 strips
15 cherry tomatoes, cut
 into quarters
1 cup HIDDEN VALLEY
 RANCH® Take Heart
 French Salad Dressing

◆ In medium saucepan boil green beans for 2 minutes. Drain and cool in ice water; strain and pat dry on paper towel.

◆ In large bowl toss all ingredients together.

◆ Chill until ready to serve. Toss again before serving.

Serves 4 to 6.

COUNTRY CORN BAKE

1 (17 oz.) can DEL MONTE®
  Whole Kernel Golden
  Sweet Corn
¾ cup milk
¼ cup butter or margarine
⅓ cup cornmeal
3 eggs, separated
½ teaspoon baking powder
¼ teaspoon salt
⅛ teaspoon cayenne
  pepper
⅓ cup sliced green onions

◆ Drain corn; add milk to liquid to measure 1½ cups. In saucepan combine milk mixture and butter; bring to a boil.

◆ Slowly stir in cornmeal; bring to a boil and cook 3 minutes stirring constantly.

◆ Remove from heat. Stir in egg yolks, baking powder, salt, cayenne, green onions and corn.

◆ Beat egg whites until stiff. Fold into corn mixture. Pour into greased, 1-quart baking dish.

◆ Heat oven to 375°. Bake 30 minutes or until golden.

Makes 4 to 6 servings.

ORANGE RAISIN SCONES

1¾ cups all-purpose flour

3 tablespoons sugar

2½ teaspoon baking powder

2 teaspoons grated orange peel

⅓ cup LAND O LAKES® Butter, cold

1 egg beaten

½ cup raisins

4 to 6 tablespoons half-and-half

1 egg beaten

FOR ORANGE BUTTER:

½ cup LAND O LAKES® Butter, softened

2 tablespoons orange marmalade

◆ Heat oven to 400°. In medium bowl combine flour, sugar, baking powder and orange peel.

◆ Cut ⅓ cup butter into flour mixture until it resembles fine crumbs. Stir in 1 egg, raisins and just enough half-and-half so dough leaves sides of bowl. Turn dough onto lightly floured surface; knead gently 10 times. Roll into a 9-inch circle; cut into 12 wedges.

◆ Place on ungreased cookie sheet; brush with beaten egg. Bake for 10 to 12 minutes or until golden brown. Immediately remove from cookie sheet.

◆ In small mixer bowl beat together ½ cup butter and orange marmalade at medium speed, scraping bowl often, until well mixed. Serve with scones.

Makes 12 scones and ½ cup orange butter.

BANANA MACADAMIA NUT BREAD

2 cups all-purpose flour
¾ cup sugar
½ cup LAND O LAKES® Butter, softened
2 eggs
1 teaspoon baking soda
½ teaspoon salt
1 tablespoon grated orange peel
1 teaspoon vanilla
1 cup (2 medium) mashed ripe bananas
¼ cup orange juice
1 cup flaked coconut
1 (3½ oz.) jar (¾ cup) coarsely chopped macadamia nuts or walnuts

◆ Heat oven to 350°. In large mixer bowl combine first 8 ingredients. Beat at low speed, scraping bowl often, until well mixed (2 to 3 minutes).

◆ Add bananas and orange juice. Continue beating, scraping bowl often until well mixed (1 minute). By hand, stir in coconut and nuts. (Batter will be thick.)

◆ Spread into 3 greased 5½ x 3-inch mini loaf pans or 1 greased 9 x 5-inch loaf pan.

◆ Bake mini loaves 35 to 45 minutes or 9 x 5-inch loaf 60 to 65 minutes or until wooden pick inserted in center comes out clean.

◆ Cool 10 minutes; remove from pans.

Makes 24 servings.

CHEESE CHILIES CORNBREAD

2 eggs, lightly beaten
1 cup plain yogurt
¼ cup melted butter,
  cooled
1 cup cornmeal
1 teaspoon *each* salt and
  baking powder
½ teaspoon baking soda
1 cup grated Monterey
  Jack cheese
1 cup canned cream-style
  corn
½ cup minced scallions
  (about 4)
1 (4 oz.) can chopped green
  chilies

◆ Heat oven to 400°. Whisk together eggs, yogurt
and butter in medium bowl.

◆ Add dry ingredients and mix until just well
blended.

◆ Add remaining ingredients; mix well. Pour into
greased 10-inch heavy skillet and bake 40 minutes.

Serves 10 to 12.

Courtesy: National Dairy Board

CINNAMON APPLESAUCE LOAF

2 cups all-purpose flour
1 teaspoon baking soda
1 teaspoon ground
  cinnamon
½ teaspoon baking powder
1 cup sweetened
  applesauce
¾ cup sugar
¾ cup EGG BEATERS® 99%
  Real Egg Product
½ cup FLEISCHMANN'S®
  Margarine, melted
½ cup seedless raisins
Confectioners' sugar glaze
  (optional)

◆ Heat oven to 350°. In medium bowl combine first four ingredients.

◆ In large bowl blend applesauce, sugar, Egg Beaters and margarine; stir in flour mixture just until blended. Batter will be lumpy.

◆ Mix in raisins. Spoon batter into greased 9 x 5 x 3-inch loaf pan.

◆ Bake 55 to 60 minutes or until toothpick inserted in center comes out clean. Cool. Drizzle with glaze, if desired.

Makes 1 loaf.

LEMON-POPPY SEED COFFEE CAKE

FOR CAKE:
2 cups BISQUICK® baking
 mix
1 cup milk
¼ cup poppy seeds
¼ cup vegetable oil
2 eggs
1 (3½ oz.) pkg. dry lemon
 instant pudding and pie
 filling

FOR GLAZE:
⅔ cup powdered sugar
3 to 4 teaspoons lemon
 juice

◆ Heat oven to 350°. Mix all ingredients except powdered sugar and lemon juice. Beat 30 seconds. Spread in greased 9 x 9 x 2-inch pan.

◆ Bake 35 to 40 minutes or until light golden brown and toothpick inserted in center comes out clean. Cool 10 minutes.

◆ Mix powdered sugar and lemon juice until smooth. Drizzle on cake.

Makes 9 servings.

PEACHY KEEN COFFEE CAKE

FOR CAKE:
1¾ cups all-purpose flour
½ cup WESSON Oil
½ cup sugar
½ teaspoon ground
   cinnamon
¼ teaspoon ground
   nutmeg
¾ cup buttermilk
1 egg, beaten
2 teaspoons baking
   powder
1 teaspoon vanilla extract
¾ teaspoon baking soda
½ teaspoon salt
1 cup peach pie filling

◆ Heat oven to 350°. In large bowl mix together flour, oil, sugar, cinnamon and nutmeg until crumbly. Remove ½ cup flour mixture; set aside.

◆ Add remaining ingredients *except* pie filling. Stir until just mixed. Pour batter into oiled and floured 8-inch baking pan. Spoon pie filling evenly over top of batter. Sprinkle reserved flour mixture over top of batter and filling.

◆ Bake 50 minutes or until cake tests done with wooden pick. Serve warm.

Makes 12 servings.

SOUR CREAM COFFEE CAKE

1 cup sour cream
⅔ cup sugar
1 tablespoon margarine or
   butter, softened
1 teaspoon vanilla
2 eggs
1⅓ cups all-purpose flour
¾ cup FIBER ONE® cereal,
   crushed
1½ teaspoons baking
   powder
½ teaspoon salt
½ teaspoon baking soda
Fresh fruit

◆ Heat oven to 375°. Grease a square, 8 x 8 x 2-inch or 9 x 9 x 2-inch pan.

◆ In medium bowl beat sour cream, sugar, margarine, vanilla and eggs on low speed until blended. Beat on high speed 2 minutes, scraping bowl occasionally.

◆ Stir in remaining ingredients except fruit; spread in pan.

◆ Bake 30 minutes or until golden brown and a toothpick inserted in the center comes out clean. Serve warm topped with fruit.

Makes 9 to 12 servings.

*H*ONEY-*P*ECAN *B*RAN *M*UFFINS

1 cup **FIBER ONE®** cereal,
  crushed
1 cup milk
¼ cup vegetable oil
1 egg
1¼ cups all-purpose flour
¼ cup sugar
¼ cup honey
½ cup pecans, coarsely
  chopped
2 teaspoons baking
  powder
½ teaspoon salt

◆ Heat oven to 400°. Grease bottom only of
12 medium muffin cups (2½ x 1¼) or line with
paper baking cups. Combine cereal and milk. Let
stand 5 minutes. Beat in oil and egg. Stir in
remaining ingredients just until moistened.

◆ Divide batter among muffin cups. Bake until
lightly brown, 20 to 30 minutes. Immediately
remove from pan to cool.

Makes 12 muffins.

CINNAMON APPLE MUFFINS

1¼ cups all-purpose flour

¾ cup KRETSCHMER®
Wheat Germ

1 tablespoon baking
powder

⅓ cup firmly packed brown
sugar

1¼ teaspoons ground
cinnamon

¾ cup applesauce

½ cup skim milk

2 egg whites, slightly
beaten

3 tablespoons vegetable oil

◆ Heat oven to 400°. Lightly spray 12 medium muffin cups with no-stick cooking spray, or line with paper baking cups.

◆ In medium bowl combine first 5 ingredients; set aside.

◆ In large bowl combine remaining ingredients. Add dry ingredients; mix just until dry ingredients are moistened. Do not overmix. Fill muffin cups almost full.

◆ Bake 20 to 22 minutes or until golden brown. Serve warm or store tightly wrapped in freezer.

◆ To reheat, microwave on HIGH 30 seconds per muffin.

Makes 12 muffins.

SNACK BARS

½ cup packed brown sugar
⅓ cup honey or light corn
  syrup
¼ cup margarine or butter,
  softened
⅔ cup creamy peanut
  butter
½ teaspoon ground
  cinnamon
4 cups TOTAL® cereal
⅔ cup raisins
⅓ cup sliced almonds

◆ Stir first 3 ingredients in 3-quart saucepan over medium heat until sugar is melted and mixture is smooth.

◆ Heat just to boiling. Remove from heat; stir in peanut butter and cinnamon until smooth.

◆ Mix in cereal, raisins and almonds until well coated. Press firmly and evenly into buttered 9-inch square pan.

◆ Cool completely; cut into bars about 3 x 1½ inches. Sprinkle with powdered sugar and additional toasted almonds, if desired.

Makes 18 bars.

CHEESECAKE SQUARES

1 cup sugar, divided
⅓ cup butter
1½ cups graham cracker
  crumbs
3 (8 oz.) pkgs. cream
  cheese, at room
  temperature
4 eggs
1 teaspoon vanilla extract
1 (21 oz.) can blueberry
  filling or topping
16 large, ripe strawberries,
  hulled

◆ Heat oven to 325°. In medium saucepan heat ¼ cup sugar and the butter; heat on low until butter is melted, stirring occasionally. Stir in graham cracker crumbs; press mixture evenly over bottom of 13 x 9-inch baking pan.

◆ In large bowl, with electric mixer, beat cream cheese until smooth. Gradually beat in remaining sugar. Beat in eggs, one at a time, and vanilla until well blended.

◆ Spoon blueberry filling evenly over graham cracker crust. Carefully pour cream cheese mixture over blueberries.

◆ Bake just until set, 45 to 50 minutes. Cool. Chill until cold, about 2 hours or longer. Cut into 16 squares. Garnish with strawberries.

Makes 16 servings.

Courtesy: National Dairy Board

Snack Bars

GOLDEN GRAHAMS® S'MORES

¾ cup light corn syrup
3 tablespoons margarine or
  butter
1 (11.5 oz.) pkg. NESTLÉ®
  Milk Chocolate Morsels
1 teaspoon vanilla
1 (12 oz.) pkg. GOLDEN
  GRAHAMS® Cereal
  (9 cups)
3 cups KRAFT® Miniature
  Marshmallows

◆ Grease rectangular 13 x 9 x 2-inch pan. Heat syrup, margarine and morsels to boiling, stirring constantly. Remove from heat; stir in vanilla.

◆ Pour over cereal in bowl; toss until coated. Fold in marshmallows, 1 cup at a time. Press in pan with buttered back of spoon. Let stand 1 hour.

◆ Cut into 2-inch squares. Store loosely covered at room temperature up to 2 days.

Makes 24 squares.

MARVELOUS MACAROONS

2⅔ cups (7 oz.) BAKER'S®
  Angel Flake® Coconut
⅔ cup sugar
¼ cup all-purpose flour
¼ teaspoon salt
4 egg whites
1 teaspoon almond extract
1 cup DOLE™ Chopped
  Natural Almonds

◆ Heat oven to 325°. Mix together coconut, sugar, flour and salt. Stir in egg whites and almond extract; mix well. Stir in almonds; mix well.

◆ Drop from teaspoon onto lightly greased baking sheets. Bake for 20 minutes or until edges of cookies are golden brown.

◆ Remove from baking sheets immediately. Let cool and serve.

Makes about 30 cookies.

PECAN PIE BARS

1½ cups all-purpose flour

2 tablespoons plus ½ cup dark brown sugar, packed, divided

½ cup I CAN'T BELIEVE IT'S NOT BUTTER!® plus 2 tablespoons melted I CAN'T BELIEVE IT'S NOT BUTTER®, divided

2 large eggs, beaten

½ cup dark corn syrup

1 cup chopped pecans or walnuts

1 teaspoon vanilla

¼ teaspoon salt

◆ Heat oven to 350°. In medium bowl mix together flour and 2 tablespoons brown sugar. With fork or pastry blender cut in ½ cup I Can't Believe It's Not Butter! until it resembles coarse crumbs. Pat into ungreased, 8-inch square baking dish.

◆ Bake 15 minutes.

◆ In medium bowl combine remaining ingredients. Pour over baked layer.

◆ Bake 20 to 25 minutes. Let cool; cut into 2 x 1½-inch bars.

Makes 20 bars.

Lemon Oat Lacies (bottom), Choc-Oat Chip Cookies

LEMON OAT LACIES

2 cups (4 sticks) margarine, softened
1 cup sugar
2 cups all-purpose flour
3 cups QUAKER Oats (quick or old fashioned), uncooked
1 tablespoon grated lemon peel
1 teaspoon vanilla
Powdered sugar

◆ In medium bowl beat margarine and sugar until creamy. Add next 4 ingredients; mix well. Cover; chill 30 minutes.

◆ Heat oven to 350°. Shape dough into 1-inch balls; place on ungreased cookie sheet; flatten with bottom of glass dipped in powdered sugar.

◆ Bake 12 to 15 minutes or until edges are light golden brown.

◆ Cool 1 minute; remove cookies to wire rack. Cool completely. Sprinkle with powdered sugar, if desired.

Makes about 4½ dozen.

CHOC-OAT CHIP COOKIES

1 cup (2 sticks) margarine or butter, softened
1¼ cups firmly packed brown sugar
½ cup granulated sugar
2 eggs
2 tablespoons milk
2 teaspoons vanilla
1¾ cups all-purpose flour
1 teaspoon baking soda
½ teaspoon salt (optional)
2½ cups QUAKER Oats (quick or old fashioned), uncooked
1 (12 oz.) pkg. (2 cups) semi-sweet chocolate morsels
1 cup coarsely chopped nuts (optional)

◆ Heat oven to 375°. In large bowl beat margarine and sugars until creamy. Add eggs, milk and vanilla; beat well. Add flour, baking soda and salt; mix well. Stir in oats, chocolate morsels and nuts; mix well.

◆ Drop by rounded measuring tablespoonfuls onto ungreased cookie sheet.

◆ Bake 9 to 10 minutes for a chewy cookie or 12 to 13 minutes for a crisp cookie.

◆ Cool 1 minute on cookie sheet; remove cookies to wire rack. Cool completely.

Makes about 5 dozen.

BUTTERSCOTCH FRUIT DROPS

2 cups all-purpose flour
1 teaspoon baking soda
½ teaspoon salt
½ cup butter or margarine, softened
¾ cup firmly packed brown sugar
1 egg
2 tablespoons milk
1 teaspoon grated lemon rind (optional)
1 (12 oz.) pkg. (2 cups) NESTLÉ® Toll House® Butterscotch Flavored Morsels
1 cup mixed dried fruit, chopped, or raisins

◆ Heat oven to 350°. In small bowl combine flour, baking soda and salt; set aside.

◆ In large mixer bowl beat butter and brown sugar until creamy. Beat in egg, milk and lemon rind. Gradually beat in flour mixture. Stir in butterscotch morsels and fruit.

◆ Drop by rounded measuring teaspoonfuls onto ungreased cookie sheets.

◆ Bake 9 to 11 minutes until golden brown. Let stand 2 minutes. Remove from cookie sheets; cool.

Makes about 6 dozen.

SENSIBLY DELICIOUS CHOCOLATE CHIP BROWNIES

1 (12 oz.) pkg. (2 cups) NESTLÉ® Toll House® Semi-Sweet Chocolate Morsels, divided
1 cup granulated sugar
½ cup unsweetened applesauce
2 tablespoons margarine
3 egg whites
1¼ cups all-purpose flour
¼ teaspoon baking soda
¼ teaspoon salt
1 teaspoon vanilla extract
⅓ cup chopped nuts

◆ Heat oven to 350°. In large, heavy saucepan, over low heat, melt 1 cup morsels, sugar, applesauce and margarine, stirring until smooth. Remove from heat.

◆ Add egg whites; stir well. Stir in flour, baking soda, salt and vanilla. Stir in remaining morsels and nuts.

◆ Spread into greased 13 x 9-inch baking pan.

◆ Bake 16 to 20 minutes or just until set. Cool completely.

◆ Cut into 2-inch squares and serve.

Makes 24 brownies.

Sensibly Delicious Chocolate Chip Brownies (top), Butterscotch Fruit Drops

Old-Fashioned Butter Cookies (top right), Lemon-Butter Snowbars (top left), Cinnamon 'n' Sugar Shortbread

OLD-FASHIONED BUTTER COOKIES

¾ cup sugar
1 cup LAND O LAKES®
  Butter, softened
2 egg yolks
1 teaspoon vanilla
2 cups all-purpose flour
¼ teaspoon salt
Pecan halves

◆ In large bowl combine sugar, butter, egg yolks and vanilla. With electric mixer, beat at medium speed, scraping bowl often, until well combined (1 to 2 minutes). Add flour and salt; beat at low speed, scraping bowl often, until well mixed.

◆ Heat oven to 350°. Shape rounded teaspoonfuls of dough into 1-inch balls; place 2 inches apart on cookie sheets. With bottom of glass dipped in sugar flatten cookies to ¼-inch thickness. Place pecan half in center of each.

◆ Bake 10 to 12 minutes or until edges are lightly browned. Cool slightly; remove from cookie sheets and serve or store.

Makes 2½ dozen.

Lemon-Butter Snowbars

FOR CRUST:
1⅓ cups all-purpose flour
¼ cup sugar
½ cup LAND O LAKES®
  Butter, softened

FOR FILLING:
¾ cup sugar
2 eggs
2 tablespoons all-purpose
  flour
¼ teaspoon baking powder
3 tablespoons lemon juice
1 tablespoon powdered
  sugar

◆ Heat oven to 350°. In medium bowl combine all crust ingredients.

◆ With electric mixer, beat at low speed, scraping bowl often, until mixture is crumbly (2 to 3 minutes).

◆ Press on bottom of 8-inch square baking pan.

◆ Bake 15 to 20 minutes or until edges are lightly browned.

◆ Meanwhile, in medium mixer bowl combine filling ingredients. Beat at low speed, scraping bowl often, until smooth. Pour filling over hot crust.

◆ Continue baking 18 to 20 minutes or until filling is set. Sprinkle with powdered sugar; cool, cut into bars and serve or store.

Makes 16.

Cinnamon 'n' Sugar Shortbread

FOR SHORTBREAD:
1¾ cups all-purpose flour
¾ cup powdered sugar
½ cup cake flour
1 cup LAND O LAKES®
  Butter, softened
½ teaspoon cinnamon

FOR TOPPING:
1 tablespoon sugar
⅛ teaspoon cinnamon

◆ Heat oven to 350°. In large bowl combine shortbread ingredients.

◆ With fork, stir mixture until soft dough forms. Divide dough in half. Press evenly on bottom of two 9-inch pie pans.

◆ In small bowl combine topping ingredients; sprinkle over shortbread. Score each into 8 wedges; prick all over with fork.

◆ Bake 20 to 30 minutes or until light golden brown. Cool on wire rack; cut into wedges and serve or store.

Makes 16 cookies.

GRANNY'S GREAT GRAHAM TORTE

1 cup (2 sticks) I CAN'T BELIEVE IT'S NOT BUTTER!®
1 cup sugar
3 eggs
2 cups fine graham cracker crumbs
½ cup flour
1 teaspoon baking powder
½ teaspoon cinnamon
¼ teaspoon salt
1 cup milk
2 cups peeled and diced Granny Smith apples
1 cup chopped walnuts, divided
½ pt. (1 cup) whipping cream
2 tablespoons confectioners' sugar

◆ Heat oven to 350°. With electric mixer in large mixing bowl beat I Can't Believe It's Not Butter! and sugar until fluffy. Beat in eggs one at a time.

◆ In medium bowl combine graham cracker crumbs, flour, baking powder, cinnamon and salt.

◆ Alternately add dry mixture and milk to batter. Stir in apples and ¾ cup walnuts.

◆ Spread batter into two greased 8-inch round pans.

◆ Bake 30 to 35 minutes. Cool in pans 10 minutes; turn out onto racks to cool completely.

◆ In medium bowl whip cream and sugar until stiff.

◆ On cake plate, spread cream between layers and on top of torte.

◆ Finely chop reserved walnuts; sprinkle over top of torte.

◆ Refrigerate at least two hours before serving.

Makes 1 (8-inch, 2-layer) torte.

WILLIAMSBURG CAKE

½ cup plus 1 teaspoon I
CAN'T BELIEVE IT'S NOT
BUTTER!®, softened and
divided
1 cup sugar
4 egg whites
1 tablespoon grated
orange rind
1 teaspoon vanilla extract
½ cup seedless golden
raisins
½ cup chopped walnuts
2 cups all-purpose flour
1 teaspoon baking soda
1 cup low-fat milk

◆ Heat oven to 350°. In large bowl cream together ½ cup I Can't Believe It's Not Butter! with sugar until light and fluffy. Add egg whites, orange rind and vanilla; beat until well combined and slightly frothy. Stir in raisins and walnuts.

◆ Sift flour and baking soda together; add to batter alternately with milk, beginning and ending with flour.

◆ Use remaining I Can't Believe It's Not Butter! to grease an 8-inch square baking pan. Dust with flour. Pour batter into pan.

◆ Bake 35 to 40 minutes or until cake tester comes out clean. Remove to a rack and let cool. Frost with orange frosting. (See below.)

Makes 12 servings.

ORANGE FROSTING

½ cup (1 stick) I CAN'T
BELIEVE IT'S NOT
BUTTER!®, softened
2 cups confectioners' sugar
2 tablespoons orange juice
1 tablespoon grated
orange rind

◆ In medium bowl beat together all ingredients until smooth and silky. Frost cooled cake.

Makes about 1½ cups.

Sunny Orange-Topped Angel Food Cake

FOR CAKE:
1 pkg. BETTY CROCKER®
white angel food cake
mix
2 teaspoons grated orange
peel

FOR FROSTING:
⅓ cup butter or margarine,
softened
3 cups confectioners' sugar
2 teaspoons grated orange
peel
2 tablespoons orange juice

◆ Prepare cake mix according to package directions; after beating, fold in 2 teaspoons orange peel.

◆ Bake and cool; remove from pan.

◆ For frosting: blend butter and sugar on low speed; stir in orange peel and juice.

◆ Beat on medium speed until smooth. If necessary, stir in additional orange juice, ¼ teaspoon at a time, until desired consistency. Frost cake; garnish with orange zest, if desired.

Makes about 12 servings.

CHOCOLATE LOVER'S CHEESECAKE

FOR CRUST:
1½ cups graham cracker crumbs
⅓ cup sugar
⅓ cup butter or margarine, melted

FOR FILLING:
2 (8 oz.) pkgs. cream cheese, softened
¾ cup plus 2 tablespoons sugar, divided
½ cup HERSHEY'S Cocoa
2 teaspoons vanilla extract, divided
2 eggs
1 cup HERSHEY'S Semi-Sweet Chocolate Chips
1 cup dairy sour cream

◆ To prepare graham crust: In medium bowl blend together graham cracker crumbs, sugar and butter or margarine. Press mixture onto bottom and halfway up side of 9-inch springform pan. Set aside.

◆ Heat oven to 375°. In large mixer bowl beat cream cheese, ¾ cup sugar, cocoa and 1 teaspoon vanilla until light and fluffy. Add eggs; beat until smooth. Stir in chocolate chips. Pour into crust.

◆ Bake 20 minutes. Remove from oven; cool 15 minutes.

◆ Increase oven temperature to 425°. Combine sour cream and remaining sugar and vanilla; stir until smooth. Spread evenly over baked filling.

◆ Bake 10 minutes. Loosen cake from rim of pan; cool.

◆ Refrigerate several hours or overnight; remove rim of pan.

Makes 10 to 12 servings.

Press graham cracker crumb mixture firmly onto bottom and side of springform pan.

Stir chocolate chips into filling.

Spread sour cream mixture over backed chocolate filling.

CHOCOLATE SURPRISE CAKE

**12 oz. cream cheese,
softened**
¼ cup sugar
1 egg
½ teaspoon vanilla extract
**1 (18.25 oz.) pkg. chocolate
cake mix**
**½ cup semi-sweet
chocolate mini-morsels**

◆ Heat oven to 350°. Butter and flour a 12-cup bundt pan.

◆ In small mixing bowl, using an electric mixer, beat cream cheese and sugar until smooth. Add egg and vanilla; beat until blended and set aside.

◆ Prepare cake according to package directions; fold in chocolate morsels. Pour chocolate batter into prepared pan; evenly cover with cream cheese mixture.

◆ Bake until a wooden pick inserted in the center of the cake comes out clean, 45 to 55 minutes.

◆ Cool on a wire rack for 25 minutes. Remove from pan; cool completely. Dust with confectioners' sugar. Serve with whipped cream and raspberries, if desired.

Makes 12 servings.

PRALINE CHEESECAKE

4 cups BISQUICK® Original
or Reduced Fat baking
mix
½ cup granulated sugar
½ cup flaked coconut
2 tablespoons cocoa
⅓ cup margarine or butter,
softened
1 egg
2 (8 oz.) pkgs. cream
cheese, softened
2 eggs
¾ cup granulated sugar
2 teaspoons vanilla
2 cups sour cream
¼ cup packed brown sugar
1 tablespoon vanilla
⅓ cup flaked coconut
⅓ cup chopped pecans

◆ Heat oven to 350°. In medium bowl beat together baking mix, ½ cup sugar, ½ cup coconut, the cocoa, margarine and 1 egg on low speed until crumbly.

◆ Press mixture lightly into ungreased 13 x 9 x 2-inch pan; set aside.

◆ In medium bowl beat together cream cheese, 2 eggs, ¾ cup sugar and 2 teaspoons vanilla until mixture is smooth and fluffy. Spread over crust.

◆ Bake about 25 minutes or until set. Remove from oven and place on wire rack.

◆ In small bowl mix sour cream, brown sugar and 1 tablespoon vanilla until smooth. Immediately spread mixture over hot cheesecake.

◆ In small bowl mix together ⅓ cup coconut and the pecans. Sprinkle over cheesecake. Cool 15 minutes.

◆ Cover and refrigerate at least 5 hours.

Makes 18 servings.

CHOCOLATE SACK

1 sheet PEPPERIDGE FARM®
Frozen Puff Pastry
1 (8 oz.) pkg. semi-sweet
chocolate
⅓ cup chopped walnuts
2 tablespoons butter or
margarine
Confectioners' sugar

◆ Thaw pastry 20 minutes. Heat oven to 425°. On floured board, roll pastry sheet to a 14-inch square. In center of square place chocolate, walnuts and butter. Pull pastry edges together, twist and turn.

◆ Place on ungreased baking sheet and bake 20 minutes. Let stand at least 10 minutes.

◆ Sprinkle with confectioners' sugar and serve.

Makes 6 servings.

CRANBERRY STEAMED PUDDING

FOR PUDDING:

2 cups all-purpose flour

1 cup sugar

1 cup milk

1 egg

2 tablespoons LAND
O LAKES® Butter,
softened

1 teaspoon baking soda

1 teaspoon cinnamon

1 teaspoon nutmeg

¼ cup all-purpose flour

2 cups fresh or frozen
whole cranberries

FOR SAUCE:

½ cup sugar

½ cup firmly packed brown
sugar

½ cup (1 stick) LAND
O LAKES® Butter

½ cup whipping cream

1 teaspoon vanilla

◆ In large mixer bowl combine all pudding ingredients except ¼ cup flour and cranberries. Beat at medium speed, scraping bowl often, until well mixed (1 to 2 minutes).

◆ In small bowl toss together ¼ cup flour and cranberries. Fold cranberry mixture into batter by hand. Pour into greased 1½-quart metal mold or casserole. Cover tightly with aluminum foil.

◆ Place rack in Dutch oven or roasting pan; add boiling water to just below rack. Place mold on rack; cover.

◆ Cook over medium heat at a low boil 2 hours or until wooden pick inserted in center comes out clean. Add boiling water occasionally to keep water level just below rack.

◆ Remove from Dutch oven; let stand 2 to 3 minutes. Remove foil and unmold. Serve warm or cold with warm sauce.

◆ To make sauce: In 1-quart saucepan combine all sauce ingredients except vanilla. Cook over medium heat, stirring occasionally, until mixture thickens and comes to a full boil (4 to 5 minutes). Boil 1 minute. Stir in vanilla. Store sauce in refrigerator.

Makes 12 servings.

Fold cranberry mixture into batter by hand.

Add boiling water occasionally to keep water level just below rack.

Remove foil and unmold the pudding.

CITRUS MOUSSE

1 (3 oz.) pkg. vanilla
   pudding and pie filling
   (not instant)
1½ cups cold milk
1 egg, lightly beaten
2 teaspoons grated lemon,
   lime or orange rind
¼ cup fresh lemon or lime
   juice, or frozen orange
   juice concentrate,
   undiluted
1 cup frozen whipped
   topping, thawed

◆ In medium saucepan whisk together pudding, milk and egg. Over medium-high heat bring to boil, stirring constantly; boil for one minute.

◆ Remove from heat; stir in rind and juice. Transfer to medium bowl. Place plastic wrap directly over surface and refrigerate until cool (about 1 hour).

◆ Fold in whipped topping. Spoon into serving bowls or use a pastry bag to fill hollowed-out citrus "shells."

◆ Chill thoroughly before serving.

Makes 4 servings.

Courtesy: National Dairy Board

FRUIT CRUMBLE

1 cup all-purpose flour
1 cup rolled oats
1 cup brown sugar
1 tablespoon cinnamon
¼ teaspoon salt
¼ teaspoon baking soda
¼ teaspoon baking powder
½ cup (1 stick) SHEDD'S®
   SPREAD COUNTRY
   CROCK®, melted
4 cups sliced fresh or
   canned fruit (use a mix of
   apples, pitted cherries,
   peaches, pears and
   berries), drained

◆ Heat oven to 350°. In medium bowl blend together flour, oats, sugar, cinnamon, salt, baking soda and baking powder. Stir in Shedd's Spread Country Crock. Using pastry blender or finger tips, work it like pastry to form a crumbly mixture.

◆ Spread half the mixture in an even layer over bottom of an 8-inch-square baking pan. Do not press down on it.

◆ Spoon fruit over crust to form an even layer. Scatter remaining mixture evenly over top.

◆ Bake 35 to 40 minutes until lightly browned. Serve warm.

Serves 8.

Citrus Mousse

CHOCOLATE MERINGUE CUPS WITH CHOCOLATE SAUCE

FOR CHOCOLATE MERINGUE CUPS:

3 egg whites
⅛ teaspoon cream of tartar
⅛ teaspoon salt
1 cup sifted confectioners' sugar
1 teaspoon vanilla extract
1 cup NESTLÉ® Toll House® Little Bits™ Semi-Sweet Chocolate
Ice cream

◆ To prepare chocolate meringue cups: Draw twelve 2-inch circles 1 inch apart on parchment paper-lined cookie sheet; set aside.

◆ Heat oven to 300°. In large bowl, combine egg whites, cream of tartar and salt; beat until soft peaks form.

◆ Gradually add confectioners' sugar and vanilla extract; beat until stiff peaks form

◆ Fold in chocolate.

(continued)

FOR SAUCE:

1 cup NESTLÉ® Toll House®
   Little Bits™ Semi-Sweet
   Chocolate
½ cup heavy cream
2 tablespoons butter
¼ cup raspberry flavored
   liqueur

◆ Spoon meringue into circles making well in center.

◆ Bake for 25 minutes, then turn oven off and let stand in oven with door ajar for 30 minutes.

◆ Remove from paper. Top with scoop of ice cream and chocolate sauce.

◆ To prepare sauce: In double boiler, over hot (not boiling) water, combine chocolate, heavy cream and butter.

◆ Stir until morsels are melted and mixture is smooth. Stir in liqueur. Serve warm or chilled over ice cream-topped meringue cups.

Makes 12 cups.

*Draw twelve 2-inch circles
1 inch apart on parchment
paper-lined cookie sheet.*

*Spoon meringue into circles,
making a well in the center
with the spoon.*

*Carefully remove baked
meringues from paper.*

Creamsicle Crunch

RASPBERRY SURPRISE

36 ladyfingers, cut in half
1 (16 oz.) can sliced
  peaches, drained
1 env. KNOX Unflavored
  Gelatine
¼ cup cold water
½ cup sugar
2 (12 oz.) bags frozen
  raspberries thawed,
  puréed and, if desired,
  strained
¾ cup whipping or heavy
  cream

◆ Line sides and bottom of 9-inch springform pan with ladyfingers, overlapping, if necessary, to cover completely. Spread peaches in single layer over bottom; set aside.

◆ In medium saucepan sprinkle unflavored gelatine over water; let stand 1 minute. Stir over low heat until gelatine is completely dissolved, about 3 minutes. Stir in sugar until dissolved.

◆ Remove from heat and gradually whisk in raspberry purée and cream. Pour into prepared pan and chill until firm, about 4 hours.

◆ Release springform pan and serve.

Makes about 10 servings.

CREAMSICLE CRUNCH

1 cup coarsely crushed
  chocolate wafer cookies
  (about 20 cookies)
1 env. KNOX Unflavored
  Gelatine
⅓ cup orange juice
1 cup milk, heated to
  boiling
1 (8 oz.) pkg. cream cheese,
  softened
½ cup sugar
1 teaspoon vanilla extract
½ teaspoon grated orange
  peel (optional)
1 cup frozen whipped
  topping, thawed

◆ Divide ½ cup crushed cookies into 6 parfait glasses; set aside.

◆ In blender sprinkle unflavored gelatine over juice; let stand 1 minute. Add hot milk and process at low speed until gelatine is completely dissolved, about 2 minutes.

◆ Add cream cheese, sugar, vanilla and, if desired, orange peel; process at high speed until blended. Add whipped topping; pulse until just blended.

◆ Pour into parfait glasses; top with remaining crushed cookies. Chill until firm, about 2 hours.

Makes 6 servings.

FRUIT PIZZA

1 sheet frozen puff pastry,
  thawed
16 oz. cream cheese,
  softened
1 cup sugar
Assorted fruit (such as
  kiwi fruit, strawberries,
  raspberries, mandarin
  oranges, blueberries)
Lemon juice

◆ Heat oven to 350°. Place thawed dough on lightly floured surface and roll out to a 13-inch circle.

◆ Transfer to 12-inch pizza pan. Trim excess dough leaving 1-inch border extending over pan edges.

◆ Bake 20 minutes or until golden; let cool.

◆ Blend cream cheese and sugar together until smooth; gently spread over pastry. Arrange fruit over cream cheese mixture. Brush fruit with lemon juice. Chill for 2 to 3 hours.

Serves 8.

Courtesy: National Dairy Board

CHOCOLATE PECAN PIE

3 eggs, slightly beaten
1 cup KARO® Light or Dark Corn Syrup
1 (4 oz.) pkg. BAKER'S® GERMAN® Sweet Chocolate, or 4 squares (4 oz.) BAKER'S® Semi-Sweet Chocolate, melted and cooled
⅓ cup sugar
2 tablespoons butter or margarine, melted
1 teaspoon vanilla extract
1½ cups pecan halves
1 (9-inch) unbaked pastry shell

◆ Heat oven to 350°. In large bowl stir eggs, corn syrup, chocolate, sugar, butter and vanilla until well blended. Stir in pecans.

◆ Pour into pastry shell. Bake 50 to 60 minutes or until knife inserted halfway between center and edge comes out clean. Cool on wire rack.

Makes 8 servings.

CAPPUCCINO ICE CREAM PIE

2 cups Regular or Cinnamon QUAKER Oat Squares®
¼ cup (½ stick) butter or margarine, melted
1 qt. coffee or vanilla ice cream

◆ Heat oven to 350°. Place cereal in a plastic bag and crush with a rolling pin or can.

◆ In medium bowl stir crushed cereal and butter together; press mixture firmly and evenly onto bottom and sides of an 8- or 9-inch pie plate.

◆ Bake crust in center of oven 10 to 12 minutes until evenly browned. Cool completely.

◆ Spoon slightly softened ice cream into crust; cover top with plastic wrap. Using your hands press the ice cream evenly into crust.

◆ Place covered pie into freezer until the ice cream is firm (at least several hours).

(continued)

◆ To serve: Remove pie from freezer and cut into 8 wedges. Spoon warm Cappuccino Fudge Sauce over each serving of ice cream pie.

Serves 8.

CAPPUCCINO FUDGE SAUCE

1 teaspoon cinnamon
1 tablespoon instant coffee
1 tablespoon water
1 (18 oz.) jar hot fudge
   topping

◆ In medium bowl mix cinnamon, instant coffee and water until coffee has dissolved. Stir mixture into hot fudge topping.

◆ Refrigerate until ready to use.

Makes 1½ cups.

MISSISSIPPI MUD PIE

1½ cups cold half-and-half,
   light cream or milk
1 (4-serving size) pkg.
   JELL-O® Vanilla Flavor
   Instant Pudding and Pie
   Filling
1 tablespoon MAXWELL
   HOUSE® Instant Coffee
3½ cups (8 oz.) COOL
   WHIP® Whipped Topping,
   thawed
1 KEEBLER READY-CRUST®
   chocolate pie crust
Fudge sauce

◆ Pour half-and-half into large bowl. Add pie filling mix and coffee. Beat with wire whisk until well blended, 1 minute. Let stand 5 minutes.

◆ Fold in whipped topping. Spoon into crust. Freeze until firm, about 6 hours or overnight.

◆ Remove from freezer and let stand 10 minutes to soften before serving. Top with fudge sauce. Store any leftover pie in freezer.

Serves 8.

GRAPEFRUIT SPRITZERS

1 (6 oz.) can Florida frozen
  concentrated grapefruit
  juice, thawed, undiluted
2¼ cups chilled club soda
  or seltzer
4 teaspoons grenadine

◆ Pour juice into pitcher. Slowly pour in club soda; mix well.

◆ Pour 1 teaspoon grenadine into each glass and fill with grapefruit mixture.

Serves 4.

Courtesy: Florida Citrus Commission

ORANGE FANTASIA

1½ cups Florida orange
  juice
1 cup (½ pt.) orange
  sherbet
2 sprigs fresh mint leaves

◆ Blend juice and sherbet on medium speed until smooth.

◆ Pour over cracked ice. Garnish with mint.

Serves 2.

Courtesy: Florida Citrus Commission

KEY WEST KOOLERS

1½ cups Florida grapefruit
  juice
1 small, ripe banana, cut
  into chunks
1 ripe kiwi fruit, peeled
  and sliced
1 tablespoon honey
1 cup ice cubes

◆ Blend all ingredients on high speed until smooth and frothy.

Serves 2.

Courtesy: Florida Citrus Commission

Key West Kooler (left), Orange Fantasia (center), Grapefruit Spritzer (right)

Fruit Shakes: Strawberry (left), Peach (center), Banana (right)

Fruit Shakes

1 cup plain lowfat yogurt
½ cup lowfat milk
2 tablespoons honey
1 cup sliced fruit (such as
  bananas, strawberries or
  peaches)

◆ Place ingredients in container of electric blender. Cover; whirl until smooth, 1 to 2 minutes.

Serves 2.

Courtesy: National Dairy Board

Coffee Yogurt Refresher

½ cup skim milk
4 teaspoons TASTER'S
  CHOICE® Colombian
  Select™ freeze-dried
  coffee
1 pt. vanilla-flavored, lowfat yogurt; frozen

◆ In blender container, combine skim milk and coffee. Cover; blend at high speed until coffee is dissolved.

◆ Add frozen yogurt. Cover; blend at high speed just until blended. Serve immediately. Garnish as desired.

Makes 2 (8 oz.) servings.

Peach Melba Tea Shake

4½ cups boiling water
7 LIPTON Flo-Thru Tea Bags
⅓ cup sugar
6 cups (3 pts.) vanilla ice
  cream
3 medium ripe peaches,
  halved
1½ cups raspberries (about
  ½ pt.)
Fresh mint leaves for
  garnish (optional)

◆ In teapot pour boiling water over tea bags; cover and brew 5 minutes.

◆ Remove tea bags; stir in sugar and cool. For every three servings combine in 5-cup blender, 1½ cups tea mixture, 2 cups ice cream, 2 peach halves and ½ cup raspberries; process at high speed until well blended.

◆ Garnish, if desired, with additional raspberries and mint.

Serves 9.

CAPE COD COOLER

3 cups boiling water
3 LIPTON Flo-Thru Tea Bags
⅓ cup sugar
1 cup cranberry juice
  cocktail
1 tablespoon lemon juice

◆ In teapot, pour boiling water over tea bags; cover and brew 5 minutes. Remove tea bags; stir in sugar and cool.

◆ In large pitcher, combine tea with remaining ingredients. Serve with ice.

Serves 4.

TRIPLE CITRUS TEA TEMPTER

1½ qts. boiling water
9 LIPTON Flo-Thru
  Decaffeinated Tea Bags
½ cup sugar
1½ cups fresh squeezed
  orange juice (about 4
  medium oranges)
1 tablespoon fresh lemon
  juice
1 small orange, sliced
1 lime, sliced
Mint sprigs (optional)

◆ In teapot pour boiling water over decaffeinated tea bags; cover and brew 5 minutes. Remove tea bags; stir in sugar and cool.

◆ In large pitcher combine tea with remaining ingredients; chill.

◆ Serve with ice and garnish, if desired, with additional fresh fruit and mint.

Serves 6.

TROPICAL MOCKALADA

⅓ cup brewed LIPTON Regular or Decaffeinated Tea, chilled

⅓ cup crushed pineapple in natural juice, chilled

¼ cup light cream or half-and-half

⅓ large ripe banana

3 tablespoons cream of coconut

1 teaspoon lime juice

½ cup ice cubes (about 3 or 4)

◆ In blender combine all ingredients except ice cubes; process at high speed until blended.

◆ Add ice cubes one at a time; process until ice cubes are blended.

◆ Garnish, if desired, with pineapple core swizzle stick or pineapple chunks threaded on a small paper parasol.

Makes 1 (12 oz.) serving.

EVERYDAY HINTS

◆ Before adding dried herbs to a recipe, rub them between the palms of your hands or crush them with your fingertips to release their flavor. One teaspoon of dried herbs equals one tablespoon of fresh.

◆ Store baking powder in a tightly covered container. To test for freshness, sprinkle one teaspoon of water over ⅛ teaspoon of baking powder. If bubbles do not form, discard it; it's old and baked products won't rise.

◆ Chill beaters and mixing bowl in the freezer before whipping cream to allow the cream to whip to its greatest volume and best consistency.

◆ When buying garlic, choose firm bulbs with unbroken skins. Avoid soft, shriveled or sprouting garlic bulbs which will have a bitter flavor. Store garlic in a cool, dry place, or refrigerate it in a tightly sealed glass container.

◆ For a different and healthful treat, place your favorite cheese or cheese spread on fresh apple rings instead of crackers. Core apples, slice them into ¼-inch rings, and dip in lemon juice to keep them from discoloring. Arrange alternating slices of red and green apples on a serving plate with the cheese.

◆ Blanching some vegetables— broccoli, asparagus, carrots, cauliflower, green beans—briefly in boiling water brings out their color and flavor and makes them easier to digest. Refreshing them quickly in cold water stops the cooking and leaves them tender-crisp.

◆ Freezer frost and freezer burn form when air (moisture) is trapped between the food and the container. Both will affect the flavor and quality of frozen foods. When freezing foods in a plastic bag, insert a straw just before sealing and draw out the excess air.

◆ Avoid "frosty whiskers" on ice cream by placing plastic wrap directly over the surface of the ice cream before putting it in the freezer.

◆ When freezing a frosted cake (or cookies), prevent the icing from sticking to the wrapping by first placing the cake unwrapped in the freezer until the icing is firm. Remove cake and wrap securely with cooking spray before using.

◆ For easy cleanup when making caramel or other "sticky" recipes, coat cooking and stirring utensils with cooking spray before using.

◆ The flavor of nuts is improved when they are toasted. Substitute toasted nuts in any recipe calling for nuts. Toast nuts on a baking sheet in a 325° oven for 10-15 minutes, or microwave in a glass plate on HIGH for 4-6 minutes, stirring occasionally.

◆ To enjoy fresh herb flavor all year, make herb oil when the herbs are in season. In a blender or food processor, combine 2 cups packed herb leaves and ⅓ cup oil until completely puréed. Freeze in tablespoon-size portions in ice cube trays or Styrofoam egg cartons. Once frozen, remove the cubes and store them in a freezer bag to use as needed.

◆ When cutting shrimp into smaller pieces, instead of chopping, slice shrimp in half lengthwise through the back from head to tail to preserve their shape.

◆ Lemons and other citrus fruits yield more juice if they are microwaved on HIGH for 15-30 seconds before squeezing.

◆ Muffin pans are excellent for baking foods such as tomatoes, peppers, apples, onions and orange shells. Foods are held upright during baking and filling them is easier.

◆ If cucumbers disagree with you, usually the seeds are the problem. Slice cukes lengthwise and scrape out seeds with a spoon or your thumb. Select cucumbers that are small, dark green and firm. Larger, more mature cukes have larger seeds and can be bitter. Add a pinch of sugar to sweeten bitter cukes.

◆ Make potato salad with "new" potatoes (thin-skinned red or white boiling potatoes). They hold their shape better than baking potatoes and do not fall apart when stirred. Add herbs and dressing to potatoes while they are still warm so they can better absorb the flavors.

◆ Separate egg yolks from whites when eggs are cold. However, egg whites beaten after they have come to room temperature will whip faster and have greater volume. Beat egg whites with grease-free beaters in a clean glass or metal—not plastic— bowl with a pinch of cream of tartar to help stabilize them.

◆ Squeeze the juice from fresh lemon halves through your fingers to the seeds go into your hand not into the other ingredients.

◆ When marinating vegetables, meats, etc., place ingredients in a sipper-type plastic bag, squeezing out as much air as possible before sealing. This allows the marinade to coat food completely and eliminates the need for stirring and turning.

◆ When a recipe calls for crumbled bacon or bacon drippings, cut the bacon into small pieces before cooking. Cook bacon pieces over medium heat, stirring occasionally so the drippings will not burn before the bacon is crisp.

◆ To separate cold bacon slices without tearing and stretching them, slide a rubber spatula between the slices.

◆ Place a damp cloth under pastry or cutting board or mixing bowl before rolling or stirring to keep it from slipping or "dancing" around the counter.

◆ When adding egg yolks to a hot liquid, stir a small amount of the liquid into the yolks to warm them gradually before adding them to the rest of the liquid.

◆ Canned fruit pie fillings taste more like fresh fruit when lemon juice and cinnamon are added.

INDEX